Anger Management

A comprehensive self-help guide to managing anger, reducing anxiety, and mastering your emotions!

Table of Contents

Introduction 1

Chapter 1: What Does Anger Mean and Why Does It Come to You? 2

Chapter 2: Prominent Types of Anger Issues 18

Chapter 3: Strategies for Managing Your Anger 40

Chapter 4: Helping your Loved Ones 80

Chapter 5: Understanding the Relationship Between Anger, Anxiety, And Stress 96

Chapter 6: Solving Problems without Getting Angry 114

Conclusion 136

References 137

Introduction

Thank you for taking the time to read this book on anger management.

This book covers the topic of anger, and how to manage it when it gets out of control. Anger can be a healthy emotion when expressed appropriately. It can be the catalyst for positive change in a person's life, and even a motivator for people to take action against injustice.

When anger is out of control however, it can be a destructive force that negatively affects a person's personal life, professional life, and the lives of people around them.

In the following chapters, we will discuss the many different facets of anger, and how to identify what may be causing your anger in the first place. Also included is a chapter on how to help a loved one manage their emotions, and appropriately deal with their anger issues.

You will also learn about the many ways that excessive anger can be addressed and managed. At the completion of this book, you will have a good understanding of anger management, and have the knowledge necessary to create a treatment plan to effectively manage and improve your anger.

Once again, thanks for choosing this book, I hope you find it to be helpful!

Chapter 1: What Does Anger Mean and Why Does It Come to You?

Just like any other emotion, anger is a quite bitter emotion that leads us to show extreme disregard and unlikeliness towards something that disturbs or disappoints us. We experience a strong feeling of antagonism and irritation because something goes against us or our expectations. In most situations, we experience a feeling of betrayal or unkind intent from the people around us that may cause us harm. Anger is mostly shown towards known people including friends, family, coworkers, or relatives, etc. Furthermore, the expression of anger is usually shown verbally. Aggression is a prominent component of anger which shows up as well in most cases when people lose their cool and act inappropriately towards their surroundings. The important question is how can we control it?

What do we mean by being Angry?

Anger is a strong feeling or emotion that shows frustration, annoyance, hostility, or displeasure. There are many different names for it; however, the meaning of the feeling stays the same. In other words, anger is an unpleasant feeling which leads to severe disagreeable consequences if left unattended. It's a very impactful emotion which has not been properly addressed and is often regarded as a temporary emotion just like happiness or sadness.

The issue with the emotion of anger is that, in some cases, it gets really difficult for individuals to control it. If not controlled in time, it can lead to extreme aggression, rage, or verbal and physical abuse towards oneself and others. The worst part about anger is that it not only harms the people around us but also leaves a negative and long-lasting effect on the person's mental, emotional, and physical health. Moreover, moderate anger can lead us to respond instantly to situations without evaluating all the factors. For instance, how many of us have responded aggressively and sarcastically towards a perceived insult through an email, only to find out that we have not rightly evaluated and analyzed the associating factors, or have totally misunderstood the message and tone of the sender?

It is impossible to say that only a certain set of people experience feelings of anger, since we all have the emotions of anger that reside within us. Each one of us has been in situations where we experience "meltdowns" or when we become oblivious of our surroundings and "totally lose our cool" towards our family, coworkers, friends, and even strangers in some cases. It happens to almost everyone; each of us experiences such situations and reacts aggressively, even the best of us. The actual problem arises when it becomes a part of one's personality and starts happening on a more frequent basis, particularly when it involves extreme levels of aggression.

Considering how you handle your anger; it can be something that can have both a good and a bad side to it. Anger, when used for a good purpose can ultimately drive and motivate you to change yourself for the better. For example, when you see something wrong happening in the society, an injustice maybe, feeling angry about that particular situation fuels your motivation to make a change in the society for overall betterment. This motivation can lead people to come together in the form of groups and peaceful rallies to either show protest against the unjust, or solidarity towards a good cause. On the other hand, when anger is used for bad, it can lead to severe consequences. Terrible things happen such as verbal and physical abuse, confrontations, and arguments that can quickly escalate to uncontrollable situations, such as extreme violence and rage: Murder. In some cases, aggression can lead to a suicide attempt as well, when one feels no escape from the situation.

Usually, anxiety combines with anger and makes a person feel miserable since they fail to control their emotions and thoughts and react accordingly. Many people lose it and physically harm the people around them which leads them to jail. Such types of incidents occur when anger is left unattended and unchecked for a longer period of time and no proper counseling is taken aboard. Prolonged and uncontrolled anger can destroy relationships with loved ones and can cause unhappiness and uneasiness among family members and friends.

The issue with anger is that most people find it hard to accept that they have anger issues, and the ones who do accept it often find it hard to control. This can happen because of many factors, such as, a person will want to let go of anger, but are unable to due to a lack of suitable strategies. Furthermore, that person might feel more frustrated about their anger issues, feeling that any attempt to get their anger under control will be futile.

Have you ever felt rage after revisiting the memories of unpleasant arguments or confrontations you have experienced? For most people, these memories can make you feel angry all over again. This is what anger is capable of. It can literally destroy your life, make you feel upset all the time, affect your health, and make you hold onto grudges for so long that you are unable to move on in life.

Anger can arise due to many factors including unfavorable circumstances where one feels threatened by their surroundings. Anger is a built-in emotion just like other emotions and cannot be eliminated entirely from one's life, however, it can be controlled through counseling, therapy, and in some extreme cases through medication. It is important to manage and control anger before it overcomes you and controls your actions and life.

The Roots of Anger?

In terms of psychology, we can relate our anger responses to our hormonal levels. Science suggests that the emotions that we feel are the result of chemical reactions in our minds that we experience, as certain hormones are released to make us feel a particular emotion. When talking about emotions, a particular type of neuron is released, called an amygdala neuron. The amygdala is an almond-shaped cluster of nuclei that resides deep inside the temporal lobe of the brain. The brain triggers a response to unpleasant, frightening, and unfavorable situations. This all happens in the amygdala area of the brain where such chemical reactions occur (Williams, 2015).

Anger also comes from stress. It can be related to anything, including personal and professional stress. Consistent stress works as an underlying agent for anger. The condition of "fight" or "flight" response refers to the psychological condition that appears in the presence of a terrifying situation, which a person can feel both mentally and physically. The fight and flight responses are activated upon the release of hormones that further prepare the body to act accordingly, either by staying and facing the situation or by running from it. This concept actually refers to the initial responses of our ancient ancestors where they dealt with danger in different environments either by fighting or fleeing. The concept of fight and flight was first explained in the 1920s by Walter Cannon in his theory where he explained the responses of animals in threatening situations.

He talked about how different reactions occurred in the sympathetic nervous system when specific hormones including adrenaline and acetylcholine were released, causing increased breathing and heart rate (Mintz, 2019).

Several prominent physical signs that appear when the emotions of anger or fight and flight appear including:

- Thoughts Racing and Rapid Heartbeat: In a fight or flight situation, your mind starts flushing with different thoughts of rage and in most cases, past experiences come to your mind which results in rapid heart beating. Your breathing also increases alongside to provide boosted energy to fuel your body to respond instantly in the given situation.

- Flushed Skin with Changing Facial Expressions: As feelings of stress and anger start flooding in, the flow of blood reduces in the surface areas of the body, whereas the flow of blood starts increasing in the muscles, legs, brain, and the arms. This may result in paleness of the face as the blood rushes rapidly to the brain. The change in facial expressions also become obvious as the changing hormonal reactions in the brain affect the facial nerves. The most obvious ones are the stretched forehead and widened eyes.

- Noticeable Trembling: In the face of danger, anger, or stress the muscles are tightened up and the body starts to shake (Cherry, 2019).

You likely have experienced any or all of these while feeling angry. More often than not, trembling is the most obvious one that you can notice while arguing with someone. As a result of the trembling, the tone of your voice changes and your body starts to shake as you exhale out the rage and anger.

There are other associated root factors which provoke the feeling of anger in a person including past experiences. Anger builds upon unpleasant experiences that affected an individual in the past. Guilt is another factor that leads to irritation and anger with time. All of these factors are interconnected. For instance, imagine a past situation where you behaved unjustly toward your loved one, but only realized your mistake later in life when you had already lost that person and had no means of apologizing. This is what we call guilt, when you are unable to get rid of something from the past and it keeps eating you from the inside, often resulting in rage and aggression towards yourself. Unless and until these hurtful experiences are resolved with forgiveness and repentance you will continue to experience guilt and anger whenever these memories arise.

The adrenaline rush, as discussed earlier, is those hormones that are released in the brain when we feel stressed, threatened, or excited. This state increases the threshold of anger in a person as compared to in normal situations. An adrenaline rush quickly releases into the body and slows down once the person feels secure and sees no threat.

Secondary Emotion – Anger

Unlike other emotions, anger is not a primary emotion, but rather, works as a secondary emotion in one's life. What does secondary emotion mean when it comes to anger? Generally, other primary emotions such as sadness and fear lie underneath the umbrella of anger. The feeling of sadness usually comes from loss, betrayal, and disappointment whereas fear derives from anxiety, stress, and worry. Most people feel uncomfortable and irritated when they experience feelings of sadness and fear. This is because it makes them feel weak and may make them lose control in certain situations. Considering these feelings, people react differently in different situations to avoid such feelings in all the ways they can. People try to avoid anxiety, failure, or confrontation through subconsciously shifting their emotions into feelings of anger. This helps them in avoiding the unwanted emotions of sadness and fear.

In opposition to sadness and fear, anger can give the person a sense of authority and control over the situation. Anger also provides a gush of energy into one's body, allowing them to feel in charge of the situation, rather than experiencing a feeling of vulnerability. These are the built-in responses and reactions that humans have. Conclusively, in certain situations, anger can work as a medium for people in creating a sense of power and a hold against uncertainty and vulnerability.

Let's look at some examples to understand what provokes feelings of anger in certain situations. When a heated argument occurs between a couple, there can be a fear of rejection underneath. In such circumstances, it's a fusion of fear, insult, and unbearable loss that can provoke feelings of anger. Assumptions and uncertainty – incomplete information about a certain incident or story can provoke feelings of anger. Assuming scenarios in your mind that never happened in reality, may also lead to frustration.

Why is this such a terrible situation for people? When uncertainty arises, people fear the "unknown" which makes them feel insecure and scared about what may happen next. Apart from this, boredom can also trigger anger or irritation since it generates a sense of fear and loss related to the feeling and experience of not doing anything productive and wasting time. While having a sufficient amount of control over feelings is good for one's wellbeing, an excessive want for control can lead to further frustration and suffering, considering it is impossible to have control over everything all the time, especially when it comes to controlling the behaviors of others around us.

Some Common Myths about Anger Issues

It is important to dispel the common myths about anger before you can change the way you think about and perceive anger, or the way you behave when you feel angry. There are quite a few myths about anger that are common to find in society and are believed by people. Let's unfold these myths about anger:

Myth # 1: Anger is Hereditary

The number one myth about anger is that it is hereditary and inherited from parents. Above all, it is believed that the way we behave is because of the inherited tendencies we get from our parents, and how we react to situations in anger cannot be changed. Many people who get angry easily often get away with it by saying that they have inherited this from their family. Such statements suggest that anger is a fixed behavior and is unalterable no matter what. However, this is not the case; anger is not hereditary or inherited. It is important to understand that people are not born with specific tendencies to express anger. The expression of anger is rather a learned behavior and just like anything else, the appropriate ways of expressing of anger can be learned as well.

It is also known that most people adapt and learn new behaviors and ways of expressing themselves by observing the behavior of others around them, particularly from those who have a strong influence in one's life. These people may include immediate family members – parents, siblings, and even close friends. For example, if children see their parents fight and argue using abusive language and violence, then chances are that they will learn the same patterns of expressing anger. This may leave long-lasting negative effects on the children but fortunately, such behaviors can be changed with time. New, appropriate ways of expressing anger can be learned. It is not mandatory to stick with aggressive behavior patterns or express anger in violent ways thinking that it cannot be changed.

Myth # 2: Venting out anger is always helpful

The widespread belief among many health professionals and laypeople alike is that anger can be reduced or controlled through screaming, running, or beating the pillow. This was considered to be therapeutic and healthy for many years. However, research now shows otherwise. A study showed that people who vent out their anger aggressively either by screaming or beating a pillow simply get better at being angry and nothing else (Reilly & Scott Shopshire, 2014).

Venting out through aggressive means doesn't help a person, but rather makes them feel more frustrated and angrier towards people and surroundings most of the time. Venting out anger is not always helpful, especially when done through aggressive means. In simple terms, practicing aggression encourages aggressive behavior. Venting out is also referred to as a "destruction therapy". This therapy doesn't help much, and instead has been shown to cause more stress for an individual. Another study indicated that such acts and ways of expressing can make anger management issues worse for people dealing with anger (Bushman, Baumeister & Stack, 1999).

Myth # 3: People Must Show Aggression to Get What They Want in Life

Many people confuse the concept of assertiveness with aggressiveness. When it comes to aggression, its goal is to show people anger through intimidation, dominance, or insult. The aim is to subjugate the other person and win at any cost. Whereas with assertiveness, the aim is to express feelings of anger in an appropriate way – that is polite and respectful. This doesn't speak in favor of harming others. For example, if a colleague repeatedly arrives late to official meetings, you could opt to respond in an aggressive way by shouting or name-calling. This approach is more of a direct attack on your colleague than an attempt to convey how frustrating their behavior is and how it affects your mood. Instead of shouting, it is better to convey your message in a polite tone and let the other person know that their behavior is anger provoking and infuriating.

It is important to stay cool in such situations and consider an assertive way of expressing yourself. You could say something like this to your colleague, "Whenever you are going to be late for a meeting please let me know beforehand because it gets really frustrating to wait every time. I hope you would consider this and regard it for future meetings". This message shows your concern and expresses your feelings of annoyance, while also conveying the message in a polite tone about what you want to see in the future. This way of expression doesn't threaten the other person, and it reduces the chance of hurting the other person on an emotional level.

Communicating with others in an aggressive way will only cause you harm and disrespect in return, whereas assertiveness will help you gain respect from others. It also allows you to not put the other person on their back foot immediately with your response. Thus, aggression is not the way to achieve goals in life, rather, assertiveness with polite delivery enables you to achieve your goals. It's just a myth that the best way to achieve success is by constantly being aggressive toward others. Assertiveness and polite behavior can take you a lot further.

Myth # 4: Anger is a 'Bad' Emotion and We Shouldn't Feel Angry at all

Anger is a negative emotion, but it does not always have a negative impact. It is not bad or wrong to feel angry. How you channel your anger matters. Anger itself is a healthy emotion, only if communicated in the right way. Numerous social injustices were met with anger, for example, Nelson Mandela, Quaid e Azam, Gandhi, and Martin Luther King all were angry about the social injustices they faced. However, they transformed their anger into positive social reforms which helped in making this world a better place. This shows that anger is not always a bad emotion. How we use or channel anger is what is important. We can always express our anger in positive ways that can bring a positive reform in one's life and society collectively.

Myth # 5: Men Show More Anger than Women

This is yet another myth that has been around for quite a long time. However, research shows that women feel equally angry as men, and there isn't much difference in the intensity of getting angry (Deng, Chang, Yang, Huo & Zhou, 2016). The only difference here that distinguishes women from men is their way of expressing anger. While men typically show anger in a more direct way by being impulsive, aggressive women often choose an indirect approach to express anger, such as by showing detachment, and withdrawing affection and love.

Usually, society encourages boys to express their anger and show dominance whereas women are often told to control their anger and stay silent in an argument. However, this is entirely a separate topic of gender socialization and injustice. In conclusion, anger cannot be associated with only men or only women and cannot be classified as a distinctly female or male emotion. It is rather a human emotion which is felt by every person, regardless of gender.

Myth # 6: Suppressing Anger Is Better than Expressing it

It is not healthy to suppress anger as it can lead to frustration. Allowing others to treat you badly, or smiling to hide your annoyance in order to keep the peace can cause inward anger. This leads to stress and anxiety and other serious health issues. Moreover, if a person continues to deny the feelings of anger that make them uneasy then chances are that those feelings of anger will build up with time. Such built up anger can be projected unfairly onto someone who has nothing to do with it. This happens because you keep those feelings to yourself instead of expressing it out in a healthy way. It is essential to acknowledge the existence of angry feelings and try to express how you feel in an appropriate manner.

Myth # 7: Anger Is All Your Mind

We often hear that anger is all manifested in your mind and doesn't have anything to do with your body or surroundings.

However, this is just a myth because emotions are physical in nature. When someone gets angry, the emotions are manifested into a person's muscles throughout the body. For example, recall the times when you got angry and had a heavy feeling in your chest, trembling hands, and a pounding heart. Anger is something that not only affects your mind, but also your body.

Chapter 2: Prominent Types of Anger Issues

Anger is a very strong emotion which cannot be neglected or ignored in any case. We all feel outraged, annoyed, and angry from time to time. As discussed earlier, anger can spoil relationships and one's health. There are different types of anger that we need to understand here. Once you understand the nature of each anger type, it will be easier for you to understand which category you fall in.

Common Types of Anger

We all face anger in different forms that we turn to when feeling threatened, hurt, disrespected, or disappointed. Anger cannot be categorized as good or bad, it is simply an emotion that exists in every person. The type of anger that we choose to express our feelings with can vary from situation to situation. Let's look into the common types of anger below:

Passive Anger

What is passive anger or passive aggression? This type of anger appears when an individual gets offended by everything. They don't like to be confronted by others and prefer not to admit that they get angry easily. Passive anger is the worst form of anger. It comes out in such ways that can exploit one's emotional and mental wellbeing. The symptoms of passive anger are quite noticeable and often shown in the form of silence. People with passive anger often become silent when angry; they keep everything inside and prefer not to share how they feel, and they also procrastinate important tasks and pretend that everything is fine in their life. Passive anger is also often expressed verbally either through sarcasm or veiled mockery. Most of the time, individuals with passive anger are oblivious to their aggressive behavior and don't recognize how their aggressive behaviors are perceived by others. This denial phase of accepting that you have anger can have dire effects on personal and professional relationships.

Furthermore, once the people with passive anger reach a tolerance threshold for unacceptable behavior, betrayals, or insults they become prone to fiery outbursts. Such outbursts usually appear in response to a triggering incident that has nothing to do with past experiences, but still becomes the reason for the aggressive reaction. This repressed form of behavior is harmful to one's emotional, physical, and mental health. For example, an angry employee who did not get an appraisal may express his anger by showing less interest in his work to 'get back' at the employer or the company. Usually, such behavior is shown unintendedly by the passive aggressive person until confronted by the management. Such people become used to these feelings and it becomes a part of their personality. They deny that they are angry when confronted by others. Another example is that a person might repeatedly try to dodge a certain situation or a person because they may not like to be in the company of that person or just don't feel comfortable in a particular situation. Such people, if forced, can show frustration and annoyance.

Passive anger can have severe consequences on personal relationships, especially between families, couples, and friends. Such behaviors not only affect personal relationships but also damage professional relationships in the workplace between colleagues and management. The question is why a person experiences this destructive behavior or what can cause them to feel this way? There are some root factors that can work as a fuel to the frequency of passive-anger.

The Upbringing:

Some suggest that passive anger is often affected by the environment you lived in or spent your life in where the expression of emotions wasn't allowed or was discouraged. Such environments affect personalities, and passive anger is just another part of it. People who are raised in such environments often channel their feelings of anger through suppressed or uncommon ways. Such people also find it normal to keep these feelings inside rather than expressing them in a normal way.

Situation:

Passive aggressive behavior is also affected by situational characteristics, such as if you live in a setting where expressing emotions, like anger or aggression, is not accepted socially, for example in a family or business setting. In such situations, people with passive anger choose to express their anger in covert ways.

Opting for the easy way:

Being open and expressive in behavior is not an easy thing for many. Passive anger can seem like an easy way to handle your expressions of anger as compared to standing up for yourself, which seems scary or difficult to many people.

Assertive Anger

One of the best ways to deal with anger is by being confident and controlled in your behavior. Self-recognition and motivation play a major role in controlling one's anger. It is important to be open to talk and listen to feedback when it comes to channeling anger in the right way.

Assertive anger can help in the positive growth of any relationship. What is assertive anger in general? It refers to the habit of "thinking before speaking" and being polite and confident about what you say. Instead of opting for an aggressive approach to convey a message, it is better to use an assertive approach. Many people show assertive anger when involved in situations which make them feel annoyed and irritated. For example, when arguing with your spouse you can convey your message in a tone that doesn't hurt them. Instead of saying, "You don't help me with work, and I don't know why I even expect it from you"; you could opt for a humbler approach and say, "Let's schedule the work and divide the tasks accordingly". This will convey your message effectively and leaves an open and flexible space for discussion. These types of comments don't hurt the people around you and also help you maintain a healthy relationship. Being flexible means that you try to be considerate and avoid raising your voice when communicating your feelings to others, and that you try your best to understand theirs as well. When you handle your anger assertively, you show that you are mature and considerate towards your relationships and yourself. Forgiveness is a crucial aspect of anger. If you get an apology from someone who made you angry and you think that this situation is not worth prolonging, then it is wise to forgive them. Being willing to forgive them and yourself for past experiences will give you relief. This will also help you in cooling down your thoughts and behaviors.

How do people with assertive anger respond to different situations? Assertive communicators always express their feelings in a clear and organized way. They advocate their feelings and opinions without violating or hurting the feelings and rights of others.

Chronic Anger

Chronic anger is prolonged and ongoing anger, which makes the person show resentment and frustration towards others, certain environments, and one's self. Chronic anger, in most cases, is characterized by constant irritation. The persistent nature of this destructive type of anger causes adverse effects on mental, emotional, and physical health. For example, the people who suffer from chronic anger literally hate the world, hate the people around them, and even their own self. In most cases, they fail to understand why they feel or behave this way, as the underlying reasons are not easily identified or accepted. An important thing to notice about this anger type is that it escalates as quickly as it arrives. Chronic anger may have harmful effects on the immune system and in certain cases can lead to mental disorders. To manage chronic anger it is suggested that you take some time out and try to identify the underlying causes behind your anger. If you succeed in identifying the root cause of your anger, then chances are that you will successfully resolve any inner contradictions, forgive others and yourself for past events. The act of forgiving one's self and others is a healing process and can enable you to resolve lingering chronic anger issues.

Judgmental Anger

Judgmental anger arises when unfavorable judgments are passed either about other people or about certain situations. It is yet again a form of showing resentment and hatred under such circumstances. Judgmental anger is usually directed toward the source of anger. This anger is expressed through straightforward, critical, and hurtful comments. From time to time we are all confronted by unfavorable situations where we feel that things should have happened differently. When we don't get the results we were expecting, or when we have to face consequences because of the mistakes of others, we shift into an irritated mode. We start thinking about how stupid and foolish we have been to get into such a situation. The feelings expressed under such circumstances are referred to as judgmental anger.

When aiming to manage and control judgmental anger, you can commit to first exploring numerous aspects of the unfavorable situation and how it occurred instead of defaulting to judgmental anger right away. You can also express your thoughts to your friends to get their perspective about possible solutions to such life challenges.

What can lead to Anger Management Issues?

There is a common misconception about anger management as many people confuse management of anger with suppression. Anger management is not about suppressing what you feel. Never getting angry is not the actual goal here, as that can be rather unhealthy for a person. A person who experiences other emotions such as happiness, sadness, grief, or excitement is also entitled to feel angry or frustrated at times. It is important to understand that anger is normal, and it will come out one way or another regardless of how many times we try to hide it. A lot of factors can add to the anger management issues, as discussed earlier, and the continuous suppression of emotions is one of the factors. Environments, specific situations, or people's behaviors can also lead to different anger management issues.

The ultimate goal of anger management is to identify the meaning behind the emotion and channel it in an appropriate way without hurting people and losing control. Furthermore, anger or aggressive behavior can be related to many other underlying issues such as anxiety, stress, depression, mental health issues, or addictions. In contrast, many individuals can experience feelings of underlying difficulties such as low self-esteem or self-confidence coupled with mistrust. Some people may also have bad experiences from the past such as physical abuse, emotional abuse, or mental abuse. All of these factors can contribute to issues with the way people manage and express their emotions, including anger.

To understand the underlying reasons for anger management issues it is important to take note of the following behavioral patterns:

- Becoming extra violent during or after the consumption of alcohol
- Struggling to compromise on decisions easily
- Not being able to come to a mutual consensus or agreement easily without showing any sign of anger
- Facing problems in expressing anger in a channelized way or through healthy means
- Avoiding social gatherings or simply ignoring people to avoid communication
- Self-harm or overthinking
- Verbal abuse, shouting, or swearing

Furthermore, if you get offended easily then you may even feel upset and get angry about constructive criticism. Receiving criticism can activate your confrontational side and may cause irritation and annoyance.

What Causes Us to Feel Angry?

There can be numerous factors that can cause anger in a person. Feelings of anger come to the surface when something goes against our thinking or expectations. The nature and intensity of anger may vary from person to person depending on different aspects: people, environments, discussions, or situations, etc. Furthermore, anger can be triggered through pain, disappointment, lack of appreciation, feelings of being unloved or not valued, and a sense of injustice.

The root cause, in many cases, is caused by tension or depression related to past events or experiences. These events may contain feelings of hurt and guilt. The fusion of guilt, pain, and hurt experienced in the past can work as eruptive anger when someone offends or reminds you of something that has hurt you in the past. Most people have the belief that hurtful events experienced in the past can be forgotten over time and won't have any harmful effects on their future. In truth though, unresolved feelings of hurt can have lasting effects on a person's future. It is important to understand that past hurts and feelings of guilt do not go away easily. Such feelings can only be eliminated from one's life if properly resolved through forgiveness and acceptance.

Recognizing and Identifying Causes:

The succeeding scenarios regularly trigger anger in people and often lead to them responding bitterly:

- **Pain of Rejection**

    One of the strongest feelings that can affect one's personality is the "pain of rejection", especially, when experienced from loved ones. Many people experience rejection either in a personal or professional setting which, as a result, makes their personality bitter. Furthermore, such feelings, if developed in childhood, can have long-lasting effects. For example, a child who developed a relationship of trust and security with his family faces a host of fears when they experience rejection from them. This creates a sense of insecurity and collapses their world. Moreover, this causes the child to create feelings of bitterness towards the person who caused them pain.

    The pain of rejection can also come in the form of broken relationships, rejected proposals, or being broken up with. Pain is related to rejection and when these both are combined, they form feelings of aggression. These feelings of bitterness sitting deep down in our memory can cause serious emotional and mental breakdowns as well. Rejection activates the same areas of the brain as physical pain. This means that whenever someone goes through feelings of rejection, they experience the same feelings as when physical pain occurs. This connection of pain and rejection was proven by a number of scientists who performed an experiment on a group of people that experienced rejection (Kross, Berman, Mischel, Smith & Wager, 2011).

- **Uncontrolled Events of Life**
Events that we have no control over can make us feel frustrated and angry. A lack of control is one of the toughest challenges for many people to face. We all go through situations where we feel helpless and regardless of numerous attempts, we still fail from time to time. This failure often leads us to feelings of anger, which affects our mental, emotional, and physical health. For example, a graduated individual who has been trying to get a job for the past year with no success may feel frustrated. The feelings of rejection from the companies coupled with feelings of being invaluable can cause depression, which is a major underlying source of anger.

- **False Accusations**
A person's good reputation is often very valuable to them. A person may feel devastated and distressed if accused of something he or she has not done. A false accusation may cost the person to lose their positive reputation among family, friends, and even colleagues.

The false accusation may have a serious impact on the life of a person, which will lead them to anger and anguish.

- **Past Experiences**

Most of us learn how to express our anger based on past experiences. We learn from our surroundings, and most of our learning comes from childhood. For example, children growing up in an upsetting environment where arguing, fighting, and abuse is a constant norm can cause them to learn that such behavior from parents is normal, and that scolding or degrading others is acceptable. The children might not know that they have developed an anger problem. Moreover, these children may grow up with hostile and aggressive behavior towards their friends, family, and other people as a result.

- **Emotional Reasoning**

People who evaluate everything based on emotional reasoning often misinterpret the meaning or message delivered. They also can consider things said by other people as a threat against their goals and needs. People with emotional reasoning issues often get offended by little things and direct everything towards themselves. They evaluate everything on the basis of emotions and become easily irritated even by simple discussions.

- **Anxiety and Stress**

    These two factors play a major role in the development of uncontrolled anger. Most people who experience anxiety often express it through anger. Anxiety and stress cause internal insecurity and vulnerability. People often release this stress under the mask of anger, as it seems easier to burst out in anger than to explain what you are really going through. Such people can be very intolerant, and often pour out their anger on other people for seemingly no reason.

How to Identify If I Actually Have an Anger Issue?

Most people who suffer severe anger don't even recognize that they have anger management issues. However, there will always be signs of anger. A person who is struggling with anger will have some prominent and common signs. Some of the most common identifiable signs of anger are as follows:

1. **Name Calling:**

    Name calling is one of the most common signs of anger. People use name calling to flush out their frustration and anger on others. It is a sign of verbal abuse that can destroy the self-esteem and self-worth of the affected people. Degrading your partner, friend, or colleague under the mask of name calling will make them feel hurt and devastated. Continuous name calling in a relationship is a sign of anger, and it can easily lead to the destruction of your relationship.

2. **Insulting and Criticizing:**

   If you see yourself criticizing every little thing frequently, then chances are that you are holding anger inside. This is a common sign of anger that you can evaluate in one's personality.

3. **Lack of Patience:**

   A lack of patience is another sign of anger. Do you lose patience easily? Do you want things to be done immediately and if not, you feel frustrated? This kind of impatience can lead to anger and aggression in some cases. Experiencing a lack of patience over the smallest of things can be an indication of anger management issues.

4. **Being Sarcastic:**

   People who pass sarcastic comments on a frequent basis are often people with passive anger. They may not realize it themselves until it is pointed out. Observe yourself to see if you are passing unnecessary sarcastic comments on everything or not. Assess yourself and see if you find satisfaction in being sarcastic towards others, as this is a strong sign of anger issues.

5. **Blame Game:**
You blame other people for ruining anything that doesn't go as planned or in your favor. Such people always put others at fault when something goes wrong, and never take responsibility.

6. **You lose your temper too often**
Do you find yourself losing your cool and acting out on a regular basis? Having trouble controlling your temper is not only a sign of anger issues but can also contribute to harmful health issues. Such chronic anger can have a negative impact on relationships, jobs, reputations, and social lives. Evaluate your patterns and identify what makes you lose your temper so easily. There are always underlying factors. It is essential to address such signs as early as possible.

7. **You get offended easily**
If you get offended by the smallest of things, then it's a sign of underlying anger. People who get offended by normal things often act out aggressively in return. Such behavior often occurs because of past events or experiences that you might not even be aware of. It is

important to identify these past experiences and address them accordingly.

8. Your anger doesn't go away easily

Lashing out in anger is not healthy for yourself or the people around you. Prolonged anger is also not a good sign. Such anger can transform into rage and aggression. Anger becomes a problem for both physical and mental health when it lasts for too long. If you think that your feelings of anger come very often and don't go away easily, then it is best to seek some professional help from a therapist.

9. Punching Objects

Do you feel any sense of satisfaction or relaxation after hitting objects or smashing stuff? If you experience these feelings or perform such acts, then chances are that you are dealing with anger. This can be due to underlying reasons such as stress, rejection, or depression. Counseling can help you to identify and deal with these feelings.

10. Overthinking and Overanalyzing

Overthinking, overgeneralizing, and overanalyzing situations and people can lead to anger. Consider a situation where you overthink about the possible outcomes and create assumptions about the event that is yet to happen. Negative energy put into these thoughts can build anger inside you and lead you to burst out in frustration without any real reason. People often make negative assumptions about others in their mind and keep on building hate or aggression for them with no actual reason.

You need to stay vigilant about your changing behavior. Identifying the signs of anger in the early stages can help you in strategizing on how you can resolve them without negatively affecting yourself and others. Self-guided anger management therapies and exercises can help you to learn ways in which you can cool down your anger. Later in this book, we will discuss some anger management strategies, exercises, techniques, and tips that could help you in coping with your anger issues. Furthermore, in later chapters, healthier ways to communicate or express anger will be discussed. Anger is a normal emotion and can be directed into positivity if channeled properly.

How to Evaluate Your Anger Levels

How can you assess and evaluate your anger levels with the aim of resolving them? There are different factors that you should consider when assessing yourself including the intensity, frequency, and duration of your anger. An initial step in managing your current anger, is gauging the concentration of your anger. This initial anger assessment and identification process is called the "rate and label" stage. You can evaluate and assess your anger levels by following the below-mentioned steps:

Step 1:

Consider a range of 1 – 10 and then decide on a number between this range which best describes your anger in terms of intensity. Here consider number 1 being low and number 10 as extreme.

To further elaborate, a rating of 2 would suggest that you feel a slight change of behavior in your emotional state, whereas, if you choose 8 then this suggests a strong negative change or feelings in your behavior which will need to be addressed properly. It is advised to choose a number honestly to define your state, as it will help you assess yourself more accurately. Furthermore, make sure to focus on the changes that you notice when you get angry such as how edgy, provoked, or stressed you feel within yourself.

Step 2:

Transform the selected rating into labels that fairly give an overview of how angry you feel at the current moment.

Consider making three different categories or labels for a range of rating. For example, you can take the range of 1-3 as one label, which would suggest that you feel irritated or annoyed.

Then take a range of 4-6 as the second label, this would suggest that you are angry and won't be able to respond rationally or logically to anyone. And, finally, the last rating range of 7-10, which would suggest intense feelings of anger that you are struggling to control. If you find yourself in this category, then this means that you are experiencing feelings of extreme aggression and rage.

How can numbers help you with your assessments in general? Quantifying the levels of anger with numerical digits can provide you with useful information in the following ways:

- Numbers allow you to identify where you stand on the anger range and how close or far you are from losing control. You are likely to lose your cool in situations where you find yourself extremely angry and mad over something, compared to the stage of just being annoyed. The numbers defined with different labels will tell you where you stand; the greater the number, the angrier you feel. The assessment will enable you to understand your anger levels in different situations and will give you some data so that you can start your anger management process.

- Numbers tell you exactly where you stand and how much a window of opportunity you may have to be able to retain control of your anger. If you find yourself at number 4 on the anger scale, then obviously you will still have some room to turn things around in your favor; as compared to starting off from point 6, where you are only a step away from entering into the zone of extreme rage.

- Numbers can provide you a basic baseline from which you can assess and measure your progress. Like where you started from and where you are at in this current moment. For instance, you might start off your anger management journey on the scale of 7-10 where you feel rage, but after applying anger management strategies and techniques you can shift down to the range 4-6 where you feel just angry, and then from there to the range of 1-3 when you only feel irritated.

During this whole process, the number at which you started and what strategies you adopt will play a major role in defining your anger level. After the successful adaptation of anger management strategies and calming therapies, you should be able to step down from your current anger level to a milder one. All you need is self-commitment, recognition, and acceptance of your anger. This will enable you to feel relaxed and at peace, once you learn to master the skill of expressing your emotions in a channelized way.

Apart from this, you can always assess your behavior in day-to-day situations. Analyze how you behave around certain people or in various scenarios. Do certain environments make you feel more anxious or furious than others? Or is there anything in general that provokes your emotions of anger and pushes you to lose patience. To be able to understand your anger levels and how it is affecting your health and others around you, it is important to keep track of such outbursts and unjustified behavior.

Another point to understand here is the underlying factors. Most people fail to admit or understand that their anger is not aggregated on its own. There are always some other factors or experiences that provide the ignition to feelings of anger such as guilt, suppressed emotional feelings, anxiety, depression, medications, or in some cases expectations from other people. These factors when left unresolved can lead to anger which can later transform into uncontrollable aggression and rage. Thus, it is crucial to gain an understanding of the different underlying causes of your anger so that they can be addressed in a healthy manner.

Chapter 3: Strategies for Managing Your Anger

In response to certain scenarios where people feel criticized, subjected, or ignored, they can develop feelings of anger and irritation. As discussed earlier, identifying the levels of anger and underlying issues that provoke such feelings can help a person to manage their anger. However, to be honest, managing anger is a tough task, especially for those who experience extreme aggression. To manage and overcome anger, there are a number of strategies, techniques, and counseling therapies that one can follow. Anger treatment can help you go through your anger problems and gain a better understanding of them. However, in seeking therapy or counseling you may want to consider certain factors.

First, anger is a normal emotion just like all other emotions that a human will experience in their life. It is fine to feel angry sometimes as long as it is not permanent or affects your health or the people around you. Second, understand that behavior patterns based on the emotions of anger are actually habits that are developed through continuous repetition and are reinforced throughout your lifespan. Fortunately, these deep-rooted habits can be changed through anger treatment. Lastly, if you plan to go for professional counseling, you can always ask the therapist for confidentiality if you are concerned about the disclosure of your information. You will have the right to a therapist-patient non-disclosure of information bond.

Without further ado, let's explore the possible anger management and treatment opportunities you may adopt.

Cognitive Behavioral Strategies

There are several different anger management approaches that a therapist may use to help the patient control their anger. Some individuals may find that their anger management improves after exploring one's self through one-to-one therapy sessions, while others may prefer group discussions or to be treated through medications. One common method of treatment is cognitive behavioral therapy. Cognitive behavioral therapies have been shown to work quite effectively for anger reduction. However, not every technique will work on everyone, considering everyone is different from each other and may respond to therapies differently. Nonetheless, cognitive behavioral techniques are a great way to start your anger management.

Understanding Cognitive Behavioral Therapy

Cognitive behavioral therapy is a type of psychotherapy where the negative thoughts about one's self and others are challenged with an aim to amend the unnecessary and unwanted behavioral patterns of an individual. It is often used to treat mood swings and other issues including anger, depression, anxiety, addictions, panic attacks, and stress.

In the treatment of anger issues, cognitive behavioral strategies help to shift the focus off of negative thoughts and feelings that typically worsen a person's anger. In the absence of such anger provoking thoughts, you can calm down, and effectively control your anger.

Some of the most workable cognitive behavioral strategies are as follows:

1. Enhanced Personal Knowledge and Awareness

Most of the time, angry individuals aren't really aware of the type of anger they experience. They don't understand what happens to them when they lose their temper or how the feelings of extreme anger take them out of their mind. If you experience anger on a frequent basis, then it is important to keep track of the events that trigger your anger. These can be small basic things such as work pressure, long lines, being overly tired, traffic jams, etc. It can be literally anything that can fuel your anger. This is not to say that you should be blaming the circumstances or other people around you, rather you must try to understand and recognize the things that provoke your anger. Make a checklist of your behavior and note down the things that make you feel irritated and lead to the emotion of anger.

To experience less anger, you might try to plan your day differently to help you handle your stress in a better way. Try to know yourself and evaluate the smallest of factors that ruin your mood. Remember, anger is just an emotion and is part of your body. You are the controller of all your emotions, and therefore you are in control of your anger. But first, you need to understand yourself, your thought process, and the people and situations that bother you. If you struggle to identify the reasons behind your anger, you can always opt for discussions with a therapist to really gain a clear insight as to what is making you angry on a regular basis.

Once you have a clear understanding of all the things that make you angry on a regular basis, you will be better prepared for them. You will become more consciously aware of yourself becoming angry when these situations arise, and you might even be able to re-structure your day to avoid those anger-inducing situations from occurring altogether!

2. Disrupting Anger by Removal and Avoidance

The techniques of removal and avoidance lead to the disruption of anger. You can simply remove yourself from a situation physically, emotionally, and mentally to avoid the feelings of anger. For example, consider a situation where you are having an argument with your partner. If the argument is going nowhere, it will be best for you to leave the situation before you become angry or aggressive. Avoidance of such unfavorable and anger-provoking environments can help you mitigate the negative energy of anger.

To avoid any misunderstandings, you can also discuss this beforehand with your partner, family, friends, or even colleagues. Let them know that you will leave the situation if a heated argument occurs, not because of you disrespect the opinions of others but because you don't want to get angry and make hurtful comments. Furthermore, it will be wise of you to seek for an alternative mode of reaction to the situation, such as writing down an email as a response once your anger has cooled down, or maybe a text message. These strategies may be able to decrease the intensity and frequency of your anger or may even eliminate your anger issues altogether.

In addition, performing some other non-angry activity may work as an alternative to distract you from the furious thoughts. Take, for example, a mother who has an anger problem, who chooses to make her planned meals for the week instead of yelling at her daughter for not completing her homework. Anger can always be channeled in alternative ways that don't include insulting people. For instance, when feeling angry or frustrated you can start counting to ten, it sounds like a very basic activity, but it can help you in distracting yourself.

Alternatively, you can go for a walk or can take a shower to feel fresh. These are some of the simple yet very effective strategies that you can follow to avoid anger. Give yourself some time and distance yourself to think with an open mind about the person or situation. Once you feel fine, you can restart discussion with a calm mind.

3. Determining Anger – Whether It's a Friend or an Enemy

Before starting off with any of the anger management techniques, you first need to understand the nature of your anger; determine whether your anger is an enemy or a friend. For instance, if you feel that someone's rights are being violated or that the situation you are in isn't healthy for you, then in this scenario your anger is actually beneficial. In such circumstances, you will want to change that situation rather than changing yourself. This type of anger will give you the courage to take a stand for yourself or to bring a positive change for other people or society as a whole.

This type of anger can be used in a positive way, such as if you see an injustice happening to someone you might want to help. To use your anger effectively, instead of acting out aggressively, you can plan and strategize a logical response to help that person. In such scenarios, your anger will be your friend. Conversely, if your behavior is affecting the people around you negatively or causing distress, then it is your enemy. In this scenario, it makes sense to improve your behavior for your own and other's sake. You might need to use calming exercises to cool down your anger. Before dismissing your anger as bad, it is important to first identify the type of anger in your life and then plan the anger treatment accordingly.

4. Coping Skills for Relaxation

The emotion of anger is often triggered or increased by threats to one's physical and emotional state. Coping skills allow you to feel relaxed in such circumstances. They also enable you to calm down the intensity of anger. The most common relaxation skills include slow breathing – breathe in, breathe out, slowly repeating a phrase or a word – something that will allow your mind to shift attention from the current situation of aggression; visualizing a place, person, or memory that melts down your anger and makes you feel relaxed; or shifting your focus to the relaxation of your muscles by intentionally pushing them to get back to a normal state.

All of these strategies will take practice. You won't be able to control your anger overnight. However, you do have to start from somewhere and practicing these techniques can help you in at least reducing the intensity of your anger. You can practice these techniques at home or whenever convenient since the goal is simply to relax. Once you master the coping skills for relaxation, you can use these to reduce your anger levels on your own or during therapy sessions.

5. Talk to a Close Friend

This strategy works like a charm for many. Having someone in your life who has a calming effect on your personality, or someone who makes you feel secure and not vulnerable can serve as positive energy for you. Talking to a trusted friend and expressing your thoughts or what you are going through can help you. Most of us fear the feeling of being judged and then refrain from expressing our feelings, even in front of our loved ones. These feelings often lead to a state of vulnerability as well. However, if expressed in front of a close trusted friend, one can actually feel relieved and relaxed. Try to talk about your issues with someone who makes you feel comfortable in their presence and doesn't make you feel judged.

Expressing your feelings with someone is not the same as venting out in anger. The aim is just to talk; speak anything that comes to your mind but in a calm tone so that the other person can understand what you are going through without feeling like you are just dumping your problems on them. For many, just talking with a close friend about the things causing them stress can help them to experience less angry outbursts.

6. Cognitive and Attitude Change

When feeling angry, many people turn bad situations into worse ones because they lose their cool. For instance, angry people often demand situations that are favorable to them. They prefer the outcomes as per their wants and the results as per their thinking or how they perceived them. Such people avoid the perspectives of others and negate anything that goes against them. People with this type of anger personality feel satisfaction from insulting others. This causes a feeling of frustration, disappointment, and hurt, which leads to feelings of anger in others. If you are among those who knowingly or unknowingly hurts people in such ways, then you need to work on this attitude since it is affecting people around you.

But how can you work on your attitude and bring change to it? The techniques of cognitive and attitude change focus on the identification of the thoughts that cause your anger, and then replaces them with rational ways of thinking. Along with the relaxation methods mentioned earlier, other attitude changing techniques can be added.

For instance, your psychotherapist might keep track of your thinking errors through careful exploration. This can help them to narrow down what your anger triggers are. Once you identify the main triggers, you can start practicing new habits or thought changing exercises for the reduction of your anger.

7. Physical Activity

Anger makes you feel furious and fills you with restless energy. One of the best ways to manage that extra energy is to use it for something positive, like physical activity. It's up to you which physical activity you decide to go with. Whether you want to hit the gym or want to go for a walk. Intense working out in a gym can help you unload the feelings of aggression and tension. Exercise has also been shown to release endorphins, so not only will you be getting rid of the angry energy, but you'll also be getting filled up with feel-good endorphins!

8. Change Your Thinking

Anger is fueled by angry thoughts and it only makes them worse. These negative thoughts are often things such as, "I can't stand this traffic jam, it's going to ruin everything today" or "Today is going to be another bad day, I already have a feeling about it". These thoughts unnecessarily create frustration. This happens because you have already made negative assumptions about the future. It's understandable that a mere traffic jam could cost you to miss an important meeting, but still it is not the end of the world. Fueling your anger with such negative thoughts does not serve you. Most of us continue to harbor these thoughts, yet they add to our anger and make it worse.

When you find yourself spending time in the fueling of negative thoughts, reframe the way you think. You can perceive the situation in a way that doesn't affect you. For example, you can tell yourself something like, "There must be some emergency or something serious that has caused this traffic jam, its' ok to wait just like everybody else in the traffic". It's a very simple thought yet it can have a positive impact. You will need to practice this on a regular basis. Try to replace every negative thought that comes to your mind with something positive and rational. It is important to keep your focus on the facts rather than on assumed thoughts or catastrophic predictions about the future.

9. Trying Out Silly Humor

Another cognitive behavioral change strategy is the use of silly humor. This does not indicate that you will laugh away all of your anger. The goal is to use silly humor, instead of aggression and hostility, as a part of anger management. Silly humor can be beneficial for certain types of angering thoughts. How can you include the approach of silly humor in your life? This can be done through looking at things in a comical way. Try to find the funny side of everything that causes you to become angry, even the silliest of things. This one definitely takes practice, but it can be a powerful strategy when used correctly.

10. Forgive and Forget

To feel better it is important to forgive the mistakes of others around you for your own sake. Oftentimes, people respond to situations unintentionally. For your own sanity it is important to let go of any hard feelings as they only burden your soul and physical state. Letting go of anger towards others will make you feel relaxed.

These strategies work well if performed on a regular basis. Just like any other regular task, you can practice these techniques on a daily basis. Start today by taking note of your behavior, attitude, and anything that triggers your anger. It's also wise to keep track of your mental, emotional, and physical health.

Stress Management Strategies

Stress management techniques are effective in offsetting the negative effects of stress that often lead to anger. Stress is one of the main causes of anger, as continuous stress can lead to feelings of irritation and annoyance. If you are prone to experiencing anger, then chances are that stress is going to fuel your anger and will negatively impact your emotional, mental, and physical health. To deal with stress, here are some effective stress management techniques that you can follow:

1. **Progressive Muscles Relaxation (PMR) Technique**

This is an effective technique that helps in reducing anxiety and stress by interchangeably relaxing the muscles in the body in a pattern that first tenses the muscles and then relaxes them. (Varvogli & Darviri, 2011). This technique was initially used in the 1920s by an American physician, Edmund Jacobson. He argued that the feelings of stress are related to muscle tension. One can simply reduce the episodes and feelings of stress by learning how to get control over their muscular tension.

It is best to practice this muscle relaxing technique on a daily basis to gain the most benefit. But how exactly do you perform this exercise and release the tension in your muscles? Physically, you will be systematically tensing and relaxing the particular muscle groups of the face, arms, legs, lower abdomen, and chest. Start off by taking a deep breath and then closing your eyes. First, place your focus on one of the muscle groups, let's say your abdomen. Tense the muscles in your abdomen as hard as you can for 10 seconds, and then release your muscles to let go of the tension. As you stop flexing, breathe out and focus closely on all of the tension leaving your abdomen.

After this, you need to repeat this process by shifting your focus to another muscle group, making sure to tighten up the muscles in that area for 10 seconds, before relaxing. This needs to be done for the rest of the muscle groups. The aim of this exercise is to enable an individual to differentiate between the feelings of tension and relaxation. With regular practice, you will become much more aware of when you are holding tension in your body and will be able to use this exercise to effectively release that tension, and to gain a feeling of calm.

When your body feels calm, it is much easier for the mind to be calm. Our emotions are deeply linked with our physiology, and so by using this exercise you can quickly and effectively reduce any feelings of anger as soon as they arise. The long-term positive effects of progressive muscle relaxation have been shown to include the reduction of stress, a decrease in generalized anxiety, lowered blood pressure, a relaxed state of mind with a stable heart rate, and the improved ability to manage one's anger.

2. Autogenic Training

Autogenic Training is designed a a self-relaxation process that one can do themselves without the help of a therapist. A psychophysiological relaxation response is stimulated as a result of this training. Johannes Heinrich Schultz was the first one to develop this technique. The main aim of autogenic training is to reduce unnecessary stress and to achieve deep relaxation which will further help in reducing anger levels. The method of autogenic training consists of a set of exercises that allow the body to relax and respond to stressful situations in a calm manner. It helps in controlling the heartbeat, blood pressure, and rapid breathing. Autogenic training is composed of several exercises that with the proper use of verbal cues and visual imagination make the body and mind feel relaxed and stress-free. Autogenic training is usually taught by a therapist who will take you through the process the first few times before allowing you to practice on your own.

3. Recognize the Warning Signs as Soon as Possible

Stress management stands on the foundation of self-awareness. It is of great importance to identify the stress factors in your life. Feeling stressed over office work or facing tension in a marital relationship can lead to feelings of extreme anger and irritation. Many of us experience stressful feelings in our daily lives so often that they start to feel normal. As mentioned earlier, stress leads to anger.

To manage anger, you will first need to identify and understand that stress exists in your life. The acceptance and recognition of stress can help you deal with it properly so that it doesn't lead to serious problems like depression and aggression. Observe your emotional and physical state to identify the stress triggering signs. Look for internal signs such as if you notice obvious tension in your muscles like clenching of teeth, sweating in the palms, rapid heartbeat, or tightness in your stomach. Your body tells you about extreme stress through such reactions. Another major sign of stress is the shallow breathing that you may experience in certain situations. You can reduce feelings of stress through meditation, yoga, and exercising. The choice is yours when it comes to the selection of exercises. Just focus on recognizing the warning signs of stress as soon as they arise, accept them rather than avoid them, and try to resolve the stress before it escalates to anger.

4. Socialize and Connect with Other People

One of the best ways to feel relaxed and stress-free is to talk to your friends and family. Socialize with the people around you, instead of isolating yourself. Moreover, when you feel stressed about something, it is better to share your feelings with your loved ones, especially the ones you trust. This will help you feel at peace and will allow you to focus on the problem that is causing stress with an open mind. If possible, try to develop friendships with your colleagues, as this can help you deal with the negative stress that you may feel at work.

5. Self-Care Is Important

It is important to take care of yourself by keeping track of activities, people, and situations that add to your stress levels. Make sure to spend at least 20 minutes with yourself on a daily basis – this will help you to feel relaxed. Sometimes it may seem impossible to step away from your busy schedule; however, it is very important to do so to clear your mind. Taking time to be by yourself can help you to process everything that happened to you that day, and also allows you to gain new perspectives on any issues you're faced with. The aim is to not to avoid stress, but rather just to give yourself some time to relax. The world is not going to end; all you need is 20 minutes off of your busy routine to regain energy. This healthy approach will also contribute to physical and mental wellbeing.

6. Give Your Mind and Soul the Rest It Requires

Your mind needs to relax in order to perform sanely in hectic environments. To gain a state of relaxation, you need to give your mind some rest. Get your mind off of work. Go on a walk in nature or a long drive to reframe your perspective about the things that are presently causing stress in your life. You can take deep breaths and focus on a positive phrase or mantra; repeat it at least 5 times in your mind. You could also pray and meditate to rewire your thinking process. No matter how you choose to find a sense of calm, the important thing here is that you regularly take time to clear your mind, relax, and unwind.

7. Diaphragmatic Breathing Patterns

Diaphragmatic breathing is also called abdominal breathing. In reality, this is the actual way through which we should be breathing. There is a huge difference between normal breathing and diaphragmatic breathing. You may have seen children breathing rapidly in their sleep, where their stomach rises more than their chest while breathing. This happens because they breathe from their abdomen instead of their chest. When we experience situations of stress, our breathing becomes fast, rapid, and shallow. This occurs as a response to the danger that we feel in that particular situation. This type of shallow breathing can become a habit, and it's how many of us who lead stressful lives breathe most of the time.

Fortunately, breathing is one of the only bodily functions whose pattern can be changed voluntarily. Abdomen breathing is a great and effective stress and anger management technique. How do you perform a diaphragmatic breathing exercise? First, find a place with minimum to no noise. Lie down in a comfortable position or sit comfortably. Now, you need to place your right hand on your stomach and left hand lightly on your chest. Instead of inhaling the air in, calmly exhale out the air through your mouth. Then breathe in slowly through your nose, making sure to keep your left hand on your chest, applying slight pressure on it. Focus on breathing all the way into your stomach. Take notice of the movement of your stomach as you breathe. Your chest won't be rising since you shifted your focus from breathing from the chest to the stomach. Practice this on a regular basis for a few minutes at a time, and take note of how much more relaxed and calm it can make you feel!

Self-help Anger Management Techniques and Therapies

Anyone can learn to handle angry feelings, thoughts, and frustration. Anyone can learn the techniques with time, patience, and commitment. Earlier in this book, we discussed the cognitive therapies and strategies that could help an individual deal with the emotions of anger. In this section, we will discuss the self-guided anger management techniques. These techniques do not require professional help or a clinical setting. The techniques that will be discussed below can be done without the help or involvement of therapists. This is best suitable for individuals who experience anger on a low to moderate level, on a regular basis. For intense anger and aggression that is causing a negative impact on your personal and professional relationships you are recommended instead to first seek the help of professional therapists before trying to use these techniques to deal with it on your own.

Techniques:

Applying the right anger management techniques can help you feel calm and focused during anger-provoking situations. These techniques allow you to reprogram your thought processes and enable you to convey your thoughts in a constructive way.

There are a number of effective techniques that can help a person in reducing their anger levels. However, not all techniques will produce the same kind of results in all individuals. Responses to these techniques may vary from person to person. Nonetheless, these self-guided anger management techniques are only going to put you on the right path towards self-control.

1. Deep Breathing

Deep breathing is one of the most recommended anger management techniques. Essentially, all you need to do is take slow and deep breaths, while trying to keep your mind clear by focusing only on your breathing. First, find a quiet place and sit in a comfortable position, then close your eyes and focus on your breathing as you breathe in and breathe out. Do this exercise for at least 2 to 4 minutes on a daily basis. It's great to try spending more time exhaling while breathing than inhaling. This technique, if practiced on a daily basis can help you enhance your ability to focus, and will allow you to gain a sense of calm when emotions of anger start to arise. Deep breathing also helps you in reducing your stress levels. Furthermore, it boosts your immunity, improves your digestion, and reduces the risk of cardiovascular diseases that are often caused by chronic stress.

2. Reducing Physical Tension

It is important to keep your anger issues under control, as they can cause serious muscular tension, causing you to face severe pain in your neck, back, and shoulders. To combat this, you can try exercises that help you in easing the physical tension. An example of one such exercise would be the PMR technique we discussed earlier. Alternatively, you could try yoga, Pilates, foam-rolling, or getting a massage on a regular basis.

3. Mindfulness

Feelings of mindfulness can help an individual shift their focus away from anger to something else. There are several mindfulness techniques that one can follow. For example, you can perform the exercise of mindful listening; enhancing your listening skills will allow you to respond to situations more constructively instead of just with anger. The aim of this exercise is to open your ears to the sounds in a non-judgmental way. It trains your mind to stay in the present and to focus on what is going on around you.

You can start off this exercise by choosing a song that you have not heard before. After selecting the song, put on your headphones and close your eyes. Your first task will be to listen to the song without any judgments about the lyrics, genre, music type, or writer of the song. Just keep your focus on the rhythm and instrumentals of the song. As you listen to the track a second time, you will need to start exploring the other aspects of the song. Even if you don't like the lyrics or overall message, try to keep the feelings of dislike aside and allow yourself to become fully involved in the music. Focus on the dynamics of the song, trying to differentiate between each beat and analyze each of the components thoroughly. After this, hone into the tone and range of the voice, see if there is only one voice or multiple ones, then separate each voice and focus on them.

This exercise will sharpen your ability to notice small details in the present moment. Practicing this on a regular basis helps you to stay grounded, and can provide a great sense of calm.

4. Exercise on a Daily Basis

Spending your time in doing any type of physical activity is beneficial to both your emotional and mental health. Physical activity can be a great way to channel your excess energy and adrenaline. There are a lot of physical exercises that you can choose, as per your liking and convenience. From simple running to cycling, to combat sports such as boxing, karate, or other martial arts. These exercises can be used as beneficial outlets for extreme aggression, frustration, and depression. Instead of venting out anger on people around you, it is better to divert the feelings of anger productively into exercise.

5. Look for alternative channels to Anger

If you believe that a situation you're faced with warrants a response of anger, the solution is to express these anger emotions in a healthy way.

When anger is communicated in a respectful manner and is channeled effectively, it can become an effective source of positive energy and an inspiring change agent. An individual can channel his or her expressions of anger through different means. First of all, you really need to pinpoint what really makes you angry or bothers you.

Think about an argument that you have gotten into recently; was it over something silly? Heated arguments often occur over something very small, like being a few minutes late for a meeting, or not getting ready for lunch on time. We often get angrier about these things than we logically should.

Before erupting with rage, first take a moment to sit comfortably and think about what exactly you're angry about, or what it is that's making you react in an unnecessarily angry manner. Identification of the actual reason behind your anger can help you communicate it in a better way. From there, you can work towards the solution of the identified factors causing your anger and respond in a calm, calculated, and logical fashion.

It's fine to fight for your rights when you think that injustice has been served to you or people around you. However, it is very important to fight fair because if you're not going to fight fair, you'll affect your relationships negatively. Explaining your rights or how you feel about a particular situation in a rational way enables you to express your opinions and thoughts without disrespecting or hurting others. Furthermore, while arguing it is important to keep your focus on the present, rather than bringing up unrelated issues from the past. Bringing up past grievances up in a heated argument is only going to make matters worse. It's better to focus on the possible solutions to the problem instead of showing aggression. The ability to react in a calm and logical way can definitely take time and practice to develop. However, once it becomes a habitual part of your behavior it can help you manage your anger effectively, and greatly improve your relationships along the way.

6. Look for Possible Distractions

Distraction is a great technique to deal with anger. It is not that you are required to avoid your feelings or emotions all the time. Rather, thinking about the situation with an open mind can help you respond to situations in a better way. To achieve this, you can adopt the approach of distraction to clear your mind of angry thoughts. This self-help approach will enable you to get control of your thoughts and will allow you to express yourself in more constructive ways at a later point.

There aren't any specific or hard and fast distraction techniques. You can basically do anything that makes you feel happy and relaxed. For instance, if cooking makes you feel relaxed or distracted from angry thoughts, then go for it. Or if you're more into dancing or singing, then spend half an hour doing either of these activities when you need to calm down. The aim is to distract yourself with something that makes you feel less angry. Once you've calmed down, you can re-visit the problem or situation that caused your anger with a clear mind and react logically rather than out of pure emotion.

7. Relax, relax, relax

Relaxation of the mind is important, especially when it comes to managing anger. Please take some time out, on a daily basis, from your busy routine to relax. This might feel like an unimportant or unproductive way to spend your time, but it can pay huge dividends in many areas of your life. Something as small as a five-minute walk in nature with no distractions can help you to de-stress a tremendous amount. Take time to understand yourself, who you are, what you want, and why you behave in inappropriate ways from time to time. Self-care is something that is sadly unappreciated by most. If you're not relaxed mentally or emotionally, you're going to end up responding to scenarios in ways that will affect both you and other people negatively.

8. Self-talk

Self-talk is a great therapy method that an individual can use without involving anyone else. Before you can help others to understand your situation or what you are going through, it is important to first understand your own thoughts and behavior. We tend to neglect our inner self and avoid catering to the thoughts that bother us. This leads to built-up frustration and stress, which often is expressed in angry outbursts. Self-discovery plays a major role in understanding your anger issues, what causes them, and how you can resolve them. Take time to talk to yourself or write in a journal each day. Jot down your thoughts and explore your emotions. Slowly, you'll gain a better understanding of yourself, what makes you tick, and why you react the way you do in certain situations.

9. Speak to a friend

It is totally fine to look for help from trusted people, especially from close friends and family members. Express your feelings honestly and let them support you through hard times. It's okay to be vulnerable in front of trusted people who you know won't judge you. You don't have to pretend that everything is okay when it's not. Keeping emotions inside only leads to emotional outbursts at a later point, which doesn't benefit you or anyone else. Share your issues with trusted people without raising your voice or directing anger at them. Let them understand what you're going through so that they can help you.

Medication or Therapy – Which one is better for Anger Management?

There are numerous effective treatment options available for the management of anger. Luckily, not every individual dealing with anger issues will need medication or clinical treatment under controlled circumstances. Most people recover through therapy and counseling alone. However, some people will benefit from medication as a part of their treatment plan. Medication and therapy can work independently or in combination; it entirely depends on the nature and intensity of the anger and may vary from person to person. To start with either therapy or medication, it is important to first identify the underlying reasons for anger. Patient history along with these underlying reasons will allow the therapist to decide on which treatment will be most suitable.

A therapist might try multiple different treatment methods in combination, as well as changing the treatment methods over time depending upon the results experienced. It's important to never self-diagnose or self-medicate. Always seek the assistance of a medical professional when creating a treatment plan and be sure to alert them if you respond negatively to any medication or treatment.

As a patient, you must understand that the treatment of anger issues or problems differs based on the situation and the person themselves. Initially, you may need to go through several treatment processes to find out which option of treatment works best for you, because everyone will react differently. The most important aspect of anger treatment is patience, and you will need to show patience during the process of finding the right treatment option you. Communicate regularly with your therapist and do your best to stay patient until your treatment plan is getting you the desired results. Remember that anger issues aren't solved overnight. Addressing your anger is a gradual process, but it is a worthwhile endeavor that will ultimately improve your life and the lives around you that are affected by your behavior.

Therapy:

Different types of therapies and counseling, including cognitive behavioral therapies, as discussed earlier, help individuals to manage and control their anger. These types of treatments work effectively, not only for anger but anxiety, stress, and depression as well. For example, therapists can develop long-term positive changes in their clients after helping them to understand and become conscious of the thought processes that cause them to experience anger. Changing patterns of thought plays a major role, as everything we do is based on our thinking – how we perceive our surroundings. A positive change can be brought about in life after bringing a change in how we think. How we react to a situation is basically the chemical reactions in our mind that are released in anger triggering situations or in environments that are unfavorable for us.

Depending on your anger levels, you may have a range of options when it comes to the mode and intensity of therapy that you or your therapist may choose from. There are different types of therapy sessions including in-person therapy sessions, online-therapy sessions, or group therapy sessions. You have the option to choose which type of therapy session you will want to start with or feel most comfortable with. You may also have the option of residential therapy; however, you may not find this option everywhere, so make sure to ask the facilitation center about this option. Once you decide on the type of therapy session you'd prefer, it's time to begin your treatment.

Let's discuss each of the therapy sessions in detail:

In-Person Therapy Sessions

In-person therapy sessions are best for those who find it difficult to express their feelings in front of other people. This type of therapy is also great in terms of privacy, as it enables you to have a one-on-one discussion with your therapist for a set timeframe on a regular basis. These therapy sessions work well for people who feel comfortable in a closed environment and can open up to one person at a time. Another prominent aspect of the in-person therapy session is that it lets you open up and share your feelings without the fear of being judged. Furthermore, the information and experiences shared in one-on-one person therapy sessions aren't disclosed with anyone else, considering the client-patient agreement to the non-disclosure of information. This type of therapy typically aims to help you view your surroundings from a different perceptive. Verbalizing your thoughts and emotions of anger with a therapist you trust helps you to really explore how you feel, and why you feel that way. It also allows the therapist to shed light on the issue from another perspective, which can help you to better understand the situation and how you might have approached it differently. This therapy session allows you to take some time out of your busy schedule to process any feelings of anger, remorse, and depression that you are experiencing.

Online Counselling or Digital Counselling Therapy Sessions

Online counseling, also referred to as "Digital Counseling", is a relatively new idea in the domain of mental health treatment. However, the use of this medium of counseling is becoming increasingly popular because of the accessibility and ease of use. People can access online counseling from anywhere in the world, regardless of their physical location. In contrast to popular traditional therapy sessions, online counseling has found numerous innovative ways to treat patients over the internet. There are numerous treatment services that can be found online. Most of these platforms have certified therapists that are assigned to you in accordance with your needs. The prices for treatment are affordable and there usually aren't any time constraints considering appointments. However, just like any other therapy type, online counseling has its own pros and cons.

Pros of Online Counselling:

The benefits of online counseling sessions are as follows:

Accessibility

We live in a technologically advanced world. Access to the internet and a wealth of information has never been easier, and almost everything is now just a click away. Online therapy is best for those who don't have access to traditional therapy sessions or who don't feel comfortable in face-to-face sessions. For example, people who live in rural areas or villages may not have advanced counseling services readily available. These people can benefit greatly from digital counseling. Internet connections are found almost everywhere, so finding counseling options on the internet won't be a problem for most. Furthermore, people with special needs or disability issues can also benefit from online counseling services. Digital counseling has proven to be especially beneficial for teenagers who experience depression and anger, as they typically spend more time on the internet than other population groups and find it comfortable to consult with people in a digital manner.

Convenience

You can find online therapies from the comfort of your home. Digital therapy is indeed convenient for both the therapist and the patient to communicate at variant times that suit them both. Unlike traditional therapies, you won't have to drive to a physical location and wait your turn. Furthermore, online therapy saves you from the hassle of booking appointments and finding relevant facilities for therapy in your locality. On digital therapy platforms, you can easily discuss your feelings of anger with either one therapist or even take a second opinion at your convenience. Online therapy sessions will be best suited for you if you feel uncomfortable discussing your concerns face to face with anyone. One study has shown that people who experience social anxiety, phobias, and feelings of fear or anger often avoid in-person therapy sessions and prefer online therapies to discuss their problems (Gedge, R 2009).

Affordability

Digital counseling has proven to be more affordable and reasonable for both therapists and patients. Clients who cannot afford high therapy fees turn to online therapy sessions, as many platforms provide affordable online therapy options. Furthermore, online therapy sessions save the traveling costs for clients. Online therapy will be suitable for you if you are on a tight budget.

Social Stigma

Online counseling sessions can help those who fear to face the social stigma that's associated with receiving any type of therapy. Sadly, many people have the incorrect belief that the person who is receiving therapy must be mentally unstable or have some serious mental disorder. This is not the case; seeking therapy doesn't indicate that you are mentally unstable or sick. Online therapy sessions allow people to avoid this judgement.

Anonymity

With the option to avoid face to face conversations, online counseling sessions prompt people to express their feelings more openly without worrying about other factors including gender, ethnicity, race, age, religion, beliefs, or physical appearance. Regardless of your background, you can discuss your concerns with a therapist by keeping your identity anonymous. The aim is to express your emotions without the feeling of being judged. This can be achieved through online therapy sessions since your identity doesn't have to be disclosed and total anonymity can be maintained.

Cons:

Along with the advantages of online counseling sessions, some disadvantages are also associated with it, and this medium has been criticized in terms of the absence of confidentiality and security, nonverbal and verbal cues, and technological restrictions. Here, we will explore some of the common cons of this form of therapy:

Confidentiality and Security

It is the ethical responsibility of Mental Health Practitioners to protect the information and confidentiality of clients without disclosing it in front of any third party. With online therapy sessions, the information shared by the clients can be jeopardized considering security breaches. Information and records can be hacked or manipulated from web servers. While a security breach remains unlikely, the possibility still remains.

Effectiveness

Some Mental Health Professionals have concerns about the effectiveness of digital therapeutic interventions. Furthermore, the absence of in-person therapy increases the possibility of a misdiagnosis being made by the online therapist. Considering this concern, some people believe that online therapy sessions are not appropriate for health concerns such as chronic anger and serious psychological issues.

Nonverbal and verbal cues

Nonverbal and verbal cues play an important role in gauging and analyzing what the person is going through during the episodes of anger or anxiety. The intensity and seriousness of anger levels are better assessed through face-to-face interactions. Online therapy sessions are highly criticized for the absence of such important factors in the diagnosis of anger, stress, and anxiety.

Group Therapy Sessions

Depending on the severity and causes of your anger problems, group therapy sessions can prove to be a great treatment method. Group therapy is a great way to recognize that there are many other people around who experience similar feelings on a daily basis. This can help you to feel less burdened and more motivated toward your anger management treatment. Listening to the stories of other people in the group and how they manage their anger can help you to gain motivation and receive encouragement in your anger management efforts.

What can you expect in a Group Therapy Session?

In group therapy, one or more psychologists lead the session for a group consisting of 5-15 people. Usually, the group is scheduled to meet once a week for a session of 1-2 hours. Group therapy sessions often involve people from different backgrounds. You get to hear the stories of other people and see the world from their perspective. You may often relate with many of them considering your own situation. The group therapy sessions allow you and all the other members to share stories or talk about what you are going through without the fear of being judged. Most of the time, each therapy group is designated to one problem type, such as depression, stress, panic disorder, anger, social anxiety, or chronic pain.

Attending group sessions can help you if you are dealing with anger problems and want to control them. Initially, group therapy may sound intimidating considering that there will be other people there to listen to your thoughts and you may feel shy. Nonetheless, psychologists have expressed, based on their experiences, that new group members feel surprised by how rewarding and helpful the group gatherings can be. Group sessions can prove to be of great support when it comes to finding better ways to deal with your anger issues. You can freely express your experiences and thoughts that make you feel angry. The other members listen to your life stories. Usually, other group members help you to find alternative ways to deal with your anger issues based on their own experiences. Moreover, regular group sessions enable you to put your anger problems into perspective. Many people have severe anger issues but only a few accept them and speak openly about them in front of other people. By observing others and how they deal with their anger problems, you can discover new strategies to reframe your thinking process and manage your anger problems accordingly.

Within the group therapy sessions, there are two types of groups: open group sessions and close group sessions. In an open group therapy session, anyone can come and join - you don't have to be an old member to sit in on the discussion. Whereas in a closed group therapy session, only registered members can participate. For instance, in a 12-week therapy program, only the members who registered before the start of the program are eligible to join in the sessions, and new members are not allowed to join in part-way through. You can choose the therapy group type as per your comfort and convenience.

Residential Anger Therapy

If you believe that your anger has escalated into uncontrollable aggression and is negatively affecting yourself and your loved ones, then you might want to go to a residential center to gain control over your anger. This is the most intense type of therapy. Residential therapy requires a full-time commitment. It lets you dig down deep into your thoughts and emotions, with the aim of learning tactics for controlling your anger so that you can reclaim your life and make a full recovery. Unlike in-person or group therapies you can't just come and visit the therapist once or twice a week. In residential anger therapy, you will be required to live in the facilitation center until you have gained control over your anger issues. This may take a month or more, depending on the severity and intensity of your anger problems.

Residential therapy has some prominent factors to look upon, such as the fact that this therapy type allows you to escape from your daily routine and avoid unwanted worries (such as your usual anger triggering situations) while you recover. Furthermore, residential anger treatment can help you deal with any prolonged grief which can turn into depression or could lead to anger, if unattended. Through residential anger therapy, people learn different skills to manage their feelings of grief and anger without becoming overwhelmed.

At residential anger treatment centers, the staff is trained and experienced in working with patients with extreme anger and depression issues. They help the patients get back to normal life by engaging them into day-to-day activities and guiding them on how to control their anger episodes. They don't make you feel degraded or less-than, rather, they help you in regaining your self-confidence.

If you think that opting for residential treatment is the only solution for your anger issues, then go for it. However, before deciding on any type of treatment make sure to consult a medical professional.

Medication

Along with different therapy options, there are medication options as well. However, not all people will need medication. The need for medication may vary from person to person considering numerous factors such as the intensity of anger, type of anger, duration of anger, and their personal history.

There are a variety of different medicines that are prescribed by psychiatrists and therapists for the treatment of anger. These medicines typically help in reducing the intensity of aggression, stabilizing mood, and help in preventing unexpected rage outbursts.

The most commonly used and prescribed medications are as follows:

- **Antidepressants**

Antidepressants are often prescribed to those people who experience uncontrollable anger as a result of anxiety, depression, or other personality disorders.

- **Mood Stabilizers**

In most cases, patients are prescribed with antidepressants as the first line of defense to treat issues like anger, personality disorders, and depression. However, in cases, where these antidepressants don't work on the patients, other medications such as "mood stabilizers" are often prescribed. These high-intensity medications are used to control and manage episodes of aggression and rage. It is important to understand that every medicine comes with side effects. These high-intensity medications often have long term side effects that you might have to deal with as well. As with any medication, always consult with a medical professional before taking anything, and never self-medicate.

When it comes to whether therapy is best for you or medication, the answer isn't a clear cut one. In some cases, therapy alone can help a patient, whereas other patients may need medication in order to control their anger. The best option will vary from person to person. This may include just the therapy or medication, or a fusion of both. Consult with a medical professional to assess your own situation and create a suitable treatment plan.

Clinical Anger

You may wonder what makes anger different from clinical anger. The difference between the two can be compared to feeling down in general and feeling depressed. In simple terms, when a normal emotion stays for too long, it turns into a clinical problem. Depression, among many other factors, is one of the major causes of clinical anger, as it stays inside the person and builds up in the form of aggression with time. To fully understand the treatment needs of a patient with clinical anger, the clinical anger scale (CAS) tool is used. The symptoms of clinical anger are measured on the CAS; items including a list of 21 statements are kept in mind while diagnosing the reasons behind clinical anger in a patient (Zaidi, 2014).

If you think you may be experiencing clinical anger, do not hesitate to seek help from a medical professional. Communicate honestly how you are feeling and what you've been experiencing, and with their help you will be able to begin treating and improving your anger issues.

Chapter 4: Helping your Loved Ones

We all deal with feelings that make us feel strong or weak depending on the severity of the emotions. For example, not getting a scholarship, even after continuous tries, can make one feel depressed and the feelings of "not being good enough" can creep in. Feeling powerless and unable to do anything about the situation can frustrate the person even more. We could feel weak and tired as a result of events that drain our emotional energy or we could feel energetic based on the occurrence of positive events in our lives. Nobody experiences only positive emotions and events – everyone has their down days. When we are struggling with negative events and emotions, it's important to have someone in our lives to depend on. Someone who can understand us and lead us through the dark alley of angry thoughts, depression, and anxiety.

In the exact same way, the people around us also need to have someone they can rely on when times are hard. This is particularly true for someone with anger management issues, as they usually experience a greater amount of negative emotions than the average person.

How to help a loved one with Anger Management Issues

It's great that you want to help your loved ones deal with anger, depression, stress, and anxiety. However, before creating a plan for how you can help your loved ones, you will first need to take a look at your own behavior. If you're not able to control your own behavior and emotions when speaking with a loved one about their anger, then you're only going to make things worse. Although your loved one might direct their anger towards you at times, try to not get too emotional, and understand that they need your help more than they need your judgement.

After de-escalating the levels of anger in your loved one, try encouraging them about the positive aspects of their personality, boost their morale and self-confidence, and help them believe in themselves. Continuous support and reassurance that their existence matters can help them to deal with any feelings of grief, anger, or anxiety in a more composed and motivated way.

Helping someone who struggles to control their anger can become stressful, so make sure to look after yourself during the process and don't let the negative energy affect you too much. Here are some steps to keep in mind when helping a loved one deal with their anger issues:

1. Keep Yourself Calm in Tense Situations

If you really want to help someone that you care for, then you will need to stay cool in intense situations. For example, if your loved one is expressing anger, the best way to diffuse the tension at that moment is by keeping calm and not showing anger in return. Losing your temper in this situation will only make it worse. Try to keep your own thoughts and anger under control and show patience. This can be tough, particularly if your loved one is directing their anger towards you. Remind yourself that they need help, and that they're not really angry at you, they're just struggling to process and express their emotions appropriately.

2. Watch Your Tone

It is important to keep track of your tone. Make sure to use a moderate tone and speak evenly. Don't show any sarcasm or judgment through the tone of your voice. Controlling your tone will enable you to gain the trust and attention of the other person, as they will recognize a legitimately concerned tone of voice and will respond accordingly. Keeping an even tone will allow you to reinforce appropriate communication. This is essential for both parties involved because if you raise your voice, the other person will feel provoked and will respond in a similar manner.

3. Listen Carefully

It is mandatory to give your full attention to the people that you want to help out with their anger problems, otherwise, they won't feel listened to and might not open up.

Consider a situation where the other person is expressing their thoughts, and no one is bothering to listen. The feelings of "not being listened to" can work as a fuel to their feelings of anger. As a friend, colleague, or a partner, you will need to show that you are listening, and that all of your attention is focused on what they have to say. But how exactly can you show that you're listening and giving 100% of your attention to them?

You can do this by following the below-mentioned points:

- Sit or stand in a position where you can see them face to face as they speak

- Nod during the conversation to show that you are attentively listening to them

- Avoid using a mobile phone, as this may make them feel that you are not focused on the conversation at hand

- Don't interrupt them while they speak. Wait and let them finish before sharing your thoughts and concerns

Being a good listener will actually help in diffusing the elements of anger from a situation and can make the other person feel relaxed and valued. It is, therefore, essential that when dealing with an angry person, listen to what they have to say and let them vent out their emotions. Do understand that an angry person might say harsh words, but very rarely do they mean them.

For an example, if a friend is having problems in married life or at work, let them vent and speak about their issues. Do not trivialize their issues, or blame them on anger or sensitivity. Furthermore, make sure to notice if they repeat any particular incidents or thoughts that seem to make them angry or depressed. Identifying the underlying issues can help you respond to them accordingly. The most important thing is to be receptive and understanding. Sometimes they may not even be looking for your advice, but rather, just a friend who will listen to them and empathize with them.

4. Do Not Reciprocate with Similar Behavior

Anger can be very intimidating at times. It is not easy to hear illogical comments and not react. But the key to dealing with a person who has anger issues is to not react. Firstly, remaining calm will keep you rational and help you understand where the anger is coming from. This means that if the other person is arguing, do not engage in counterargument. But this does not mean to totally ignore the angry person, as this will only escalate the behavior and increase its chances of repeating itself. On the contrary, use self-restraint and remain calm and cool. Let the angry phase pass through neutralizing sentences like, "I understand how you feel" and "I empathize with you". Let the storm pass.

5. Show Concern and Compassion

Most of the time, our loved ones feel angry because they think that they are not being understood or heard. If you plan to help your loved ones, make sure that they don't feel unheard. Make sure they understand that you are there for them, and that you are truly listening to what they say. Show, through your talk and gestures, that you are taking them seriously and actually value their thoughts, feelings, and opinions. By showing concern and compassion, you can gain their trust and allow them to feel understood, valued, and cared about.

Show your support and compassion by responding with understanding comments, such as:

- "I can see why you feel frustrated and angry about what happened".

- "After listening to what you have been through, I can totally understand your anger".

- "I believe I understand your problem; I've been in a similar situation as well".

Making it clear that you are there to help without judgement will assist in reducing their anger. Once you are able to engage them in a normal conversation, try to share your own experiences and struggles and how you overcame them.

Empathize with them, and let them know that you're always there for them if they need your help.

6. Mark your Boundaries

In the process of helping others, don't forget about your own wellbeing. Make it clear that you are here to help without any ulterior motives; however, the one thing that you expect in return, is respect. It is important that you make this clear from the outset. Don't let your loved ones treat you with disrespect. It is understandable that they might lose their anger during the conversation and try to dump their frustration on you. Even if it is your intimate partner, your parent, your coworker, boss, or any such person, you do not always have to accept unjustified behavior for the sake of saving relationships. Enact boundaries from the start and maintain them. Dealing with an angry person and helping them deal with anger issues does not mean that the helper should be exposed to disrespect or anxiety. Make ground rules that if you are disrespected during a conversation where you're trying to help, you will disengage, and the conversation will end for the time being.

You can always say something like, "I'm sorry but I'll have to leave if you don't stop shouting", or "I believe I should leave and continue this discussion some other time", or even "I am afraid I'll have to leave this conversation here if you don't stop with the unnecessary aggression towards me".

Avoid getting angry and shouting in response, otherwise, it will only increase the intensity of the situation and make matters worse. Set your boundaries and make them clear to your loved ones. Once it's clear, you can communicate in a moderate and understanding tone as discussed earlier.

You can mark your boundaries by making statements like, "I respect your feelings and what you have to say, and I ask that you show me the same courtesy". This is a statement of assurance. Now that you have shown that you trust them and will show them respect, it's more likely that they will act in a similar manner.

7. The Calm Talk

After the angry person has shared their feelings and has calmed down, have a conversation about their issues in a calm and cool manner. Discuss the reasons for their anger and let them know how it is making you or other people interacting with them feel. This aim of this talk is to let them know that you are here to support them and help in finding solutions to their anger issues. Also, you can use the calm talk to decide on the strategies that both of you may want to use when dealing with future anger outbursts. Together, you can discuss treatment options, and develop a plan for improving the situation.

8. Make sure to use "I" in your statements when discussing the problem

To avoid making the person feel too much blame and shame, it is better to use "I" when explaining your point of view. Try to convey your message or needs in a calm tone without blaming the other person. Furthermore, when dealing with an angry person you can explain the situations by applying them to yourself. For example, you can say something like, "I have been through a similar situation and trust me I know how you feel". When expressing your concerns during an argument, you can always state your point of view in a way that it doesn't add to the heat of the moment. For instance, instead of saying something like, "You have to stop shouting at me!" you can convey your message by saying, "It makes me feel scared and nervous when you shout at me, can we talk nicely to one another?"

9. Don't rush into suggestions or advice

When dealing with an angry person, don't try to give too much advice and fix all of their problems. Even constructive criticism may offend them in such situations. Most of the time, they just need someone to listen to their issues, and empathize with them. If you really want to help a loved one, then let them speak and express what they are going through without any interruption. Listen carefully to everything they say before giving them any suggestion, advice, or solution.

Once they are done talking, you can ask questions like:

"Do you want me to help you out with your situation or did you just want to express what you are going through?"
Or you can say something like, "I understand your situation, do you want my help? How can I help you?"

Furthermore, if you feel like the other person is in a bad mood and won't be receptive to discussing or listen to anything at all, then leave the solutions and questions for another day when they are in a better mood.

10. Take a break

It's hard to help a loved one if you don't feel fine yourself or are dealing with your own issues. If you feel overwhelmed, take some time to look after yourself before helping everyone else.
When trying to help a loved one, make sure to excuse yourself from any situation where you feel uncomfortable. You can excuse yourself by saying something like, "I don't think we are going to come up with a solution if we keep fighting unreasonably like this. Let's take a moment here and relax, okay?"

11. Focus on the problem rather than the person

It is best to pay attention to the underlying issues when your loved one is sharing their feelings with you during a conversation. Your aim should be to take note of the things that make the other person angry. Notice if there are any points or names that they repeat while venting out their anger. This approach will enable you to better understand the cause of their anger, and plan an anger management strategy that will focus on those points that need the most attention. Moreover, in a conversation with an angry person, specifically, a loved one, make sure to convey to them that their behavior is affecting you. Remind them in a concerned way so that it doesn't sound like they are the problem. This may increase the chances of their cooperation with you.

Controlling or Managing Anger in a Marriage

It is hard to spend your life with someone who has serious anger management issues. Being angry all the time not only makes life exhausting for the person who is angry, but it also drains the energy from people around them, especially in a marriage where you spend a large amount of time together. To make matters worse, people who have anger management issues typically have difficulty managing their other emotions as well.

Dealing with a partner with anger problems in a marriage, can be a long and trying process. It is, however, necessary to work on these anger issues in an appropriate way. If approached incorrectly, it can affect your relationship permanently with that person. It is recommended to create and follow a plan to control and manage your or your partner's anger so that it doesn't affect your relationship negatively.

In a relationship, you must also keep in mind that the reason behind the anger of your partner is not always you. Even though it may seem like their anger is being directed towards you, it can be caused initially by just about anything. In the same manner, you are not responsible for mending or managing your partner all the time. However, you can always work together to help them understand their behavior and show them how their angry behavior is affecting you. It must also be considered that anger management is not about suppressing or crushing the anger, it is about understanding and controlling the anger. How both partners control and manage their anger depends on numerous factors such as their will to change or improve their lifestyle and behavior. If you are the one who plans to help your partner with anger management issues, then your goal should be to help that person understand the consequences of their behavior and how they can control their anger.

When dealing with a partner who has anger issues, it's good to keep the following things in mind:

1. Know When it's Time to Leave

It is important that strategies to deal with a person with anger issues should focus on helping the person mitigate their anger through understanding the root cause, as well as the dynamics of the stressors causing the anger. However, if the situation gets so dangerous that the angry person is a threat physically or psychology to the well-being of others, one should leave the conversation, room, or the relationship if necessary. In such situations, disengagement from a risky situation is the right decision to make. This becomes more essential in situations where an intimate partner is involved, as evidence shows that unaddressed anger issues often escalate to violence between partners. In such a situation, if signs of anger escalation are sensed and you feel unsafe, then it is of utmost importance to leave the situation and find a safe environment.

2. Don't Depend too Much on the Triangle

After having a heated argument with your partner, you may feel like talking to a friend, your children, or sometimes even with your therapist (if you are seeing one). The process of going to a third person for managing the stress caused by a situation or our partner is called an emotion triangle. It is normal to vent our frustrations in front of someone whom we trust; however, this process of "Triangling" often gets us off track from solving the problems in the original relationship. At times, going to a third person can actually make things worse. For example, it can cause your partner to feel even angrier, isolated, or more defensive considering that you have been sharing personal things with others. Thus, it is important to act wisely and not share your personal information with your friends after every little disagreement. Next time you decide to call a friend to complain to about your partner, ask yourself this first:

"Am I really looking for someone to help me? Or Do I just want another person to agree with me?"

If it's the latter, then it is best to calm yourself and discuss the situation with your partner in an open, honest, and concerned way.

3. Try to Look Past Triggering Topics of Conversation

As individuals, there are certain discussion topics that trigger our anger and lead us to serious conflicts. These topics often include money, love, family, religion, sex, or politics. It is a common assumption that different opinions and views lead to conflict or anger, whereas, in reality, it's usually the immature reactions that people have in certain situations that cause issues. So, instead of defaulting to anger when one of these topics arises in conversation, it is best to act and respond as logically and maturely to the situation as possible. Listen to your partner's point of view and try to understand where they are coming from. Share your own opinions and feelings in a calm and respectful way, and ask that they also try and see things from your perspective.

If you feel like you are being overwhelmed by your relationship, then remind yourself that you are 50% of it. If you can act maturely and in a calm manner, then the chances that your relationship will become more stable increase. This approach may make your partner realize their unnecessary anger, and they may start to act more maturely. Or if that fails, you will likely realize in the process that this relationship isn't right for your emotional and mental health. Whatever the case may be, act maturely and logically, and choose to not let your aggressive feelings take over a conversation.

4. Avoid Impulsive Reactions

Sometimes when you are in an argument with your partner, you may feel the strong urge to show aggression physically, either by shouting or slamming the door, or even by going silent in a fight. The silent treatment may sound good to you but will only work as a temporary escape, because the chances are that it's only going to add to the anger and anxiety of the other person. This does not mean that you have to respond to the problem instantly or to work out the situation right then and there. Instead of acting aggressively or allowing the situation to escalate further, it is best to simply excuse yourself from the situation for a while until you've both calmed down. Tell your partner that you need to think about this discussion and need some time. This will also give some time for your partner to do the same. Revisit the topic of discussion when you've both calm and have had time to think the issue over.

5. Get Help

Even after trying to help a loved one deal with anger management issues on your own, it's always best to seek professional help. Although you cannot force or make a person seek help to deal with their anger issues, you can communicate to them that it is essential for their and others wellbeing. There are many therapists, classes, and courses as discussed in an earlier chapter that can help the person with anger management issues to manage their anger effectively. It's definitely possible to improve your relationship and help your partner with their issues on your own. However, the best results will come from involving a professional who can properly diagnose your partner, and design a suitable treatment plan for them.

Chapter 5: Understanding the Relationship Between Anger, Anxiety, And Stress

Human emotions are often so intricately intertwined together that it becomes difficult to demarcate a line from where one emotion ends and the other starts. It is often one emotion that triggers the other and the ball keeps rolling. Grief, stress, anxiety, and anger; they are so different yet so similar, and it can be complicated at times to point out which one a person is experiencing as they often lead to similar reactions.

As it was discussed before, anger is often a secondary emotion, worn like a mask to hide the other emotions underneath which make a person feel vulnerable. Anxiety and stress are among the emotions which can make a person feel vulnerable, hence they are often sheltered by anger.

The Relation between Anger and Stress

To understand the relationship that exists between anger, anxiety, and stress, it is important to understand each of these emotions individually. Have you ever noticed how stress leads you to anger? Stress has become increasingly prevalent in the world today and is often worn like a badge of honor by productive and ambitious people. However, this increase in stress isn't healthy, and as a result has also led to an increase in anger. Workplace aggression and road rage are two of the very common expressions of anger that we can commonly observe in everyday life.

So, what is stress exactly? In a more literal context, it means exerting pressure on an object. That pressure obviously has to be physical in order to be exerted on a material object; however, when this pressure is in the form of demanding circumstances, it exerts itself on a person's mental and emotional state, leading to human stress. Stress is not always entirely unhealthy. It's healthy stress which forces us to take charge of our daily routine and become productive. It makes people ambitious and drives them to perform better in their professional lives. However, when the emotion of stress gets too large to bare, it often transitions into anger. At this point, stress no longer serves as a motivator, and has a negative impact rather than a positive one. This kind of stress is also referred to as "Distress".

It is often little things around us that we fail to notice, which prove to be the underlying causes of our stress. These little things may seem trivial individually, but they can add up and lead to feelings of overwhelm and helplessness. When a person feels stressed, the foremost thing to do is to analyze the environment that the person is surrounded by. Is the work or home environment too chaotic? Is the workload more than they can take? Is there a healthy balance between work and home life? Investigating these areas of life can help an individual to identify the things causing their stress.

Now if these things are causing stress to a person, how exactly are these factors related to anger?

As mentioned earlier, anger is often used to cover up our other emotions. For example, anger can be caused by feelings of inadequacy, overwhelm, anxiety, depression, or stress, to name a few. Rather than asking for help when feeling stressed or talking to someone about the stress they are experiencing, many people resort to lashing out in anger. Some of the time, a person might not have even identified their stressors, and not be consciously aware of what is causing them to be angry in the first place. That's why it's important for people to examine their environment and identify if they have an unhealthy amount of stress their lives. From there, strategies can be put in place to lower that stress, and ultimately, their anger.

The Relationship between Anger and Anxiety

Anxiety and anger are typically viewed as two very different emotions, however, they are often intertwined and can have quite an effect on one another.

While the concept of anger has been discussed in much detail, what exactly is anxiety? Have you felt uneasy about something that has yet to happen and you don't know how will it go? Or maybe you know what will happen, and the thought how people will react to it is what makes you feel uneasy? This feeling of uneasiness is "Anxiety". It's a combination of stress, fear, and a consequent lack of focus. It can have severe symptoms, such as sweating, depression, and even weight gain and blood pressure problems in the long run. Oftentimes, anxiety is an underlying factor of anger. Feelings of frustration are built upon thoughts that are filled with anxiety. The role of anger cannot be ignored in most of the anxiety disorders, including "Generalized Anxiety Disorder", where it is common for anger to be used to cover up feelings of anxiety.

Anger can serve as an aggravating factor for the symptoms that lead to Generalized Anxiety Disorder, and this very fact has been proved through research conducted at Concordia University. There are different symptoms that are common among the emotions that link them together. As has been mentioned multiple times, "irritability" is strongly associated with anger, and it also happens to be a diagnostic feature of Anxiety Disorder. Uncontrollable and excessive worry over everything leads to irritability, which magnifies to take the shape of anger. Those who suffer from anxiety are more vulnerable to anticipating disaster and will fret over everyday issues more than the average person, including issues such as work, studies, money, health, and relationships. This anticipation of disaster in every aspect brings fear of loss which can breed anger.

The bond between anger and anxiety is quite a complicated and tightly intertwined one where it is tough to identify which emotion affects which. Adding on to the research by Concordia University that showed that anger aggravates the indicators of nervousness, it was determined by the researchers that some of the most prominent components of anger which include physical and verbal aggression, hostility, and an expression of anger, contribute significantly to anxiety.

How Is Stress Different from The Rest?

A major reason why an individual may feel stressed is due to the presence of stressors in the environment; however, it also has to do with what an individual tends to imagine in his/her mind about the consequences of a certain future event.

Stress is not just one emotion that affects everyone in the same way. There may be someone in a class who maintains a normal routine, prepares a little, and then takes a test. On the other hand, there may be someone in the same class who will lose multiple nights of sleep preparing or worrying about the same test. The test, in this case, is the obvious stressor at hand, but there are different underlying factors that will cause people to react to it differently. For example, the first student might be the only child of the family and have great support from their family with regards to their studies and results; while the latter might be scolded regularly for scoring less than their sibling, causing increased pressure to perform at school. This will obviously lead to them being more anxious, and more stressed than the other student, causing them to lose sleep worrying and preparing.

In order to understand how stress is different from other emotions, it is important to learn about the two common types of stress that individuals experience:

Acute Stress

What people face most commonly is acute stress. When demands of the near future and unmet demands of the near past combine, they lead to acute stress, which can be exciting when it comes in small bouts; however, it can also be frustrating and exhausting when it piles up. Fortunately, acute stress is easily recognizable. When affected by acute stress, a person may be feeling emotionally distressed, have muscular aches, stomach problems, or a temporary rise in blood pressure, to name a few symptoms. Fortunately, acute stress does not cause long-term damage.

Episodic Acute Stress

When acute stress becomes a frequent part of everyday life as a result of increased pressure in one or more areas of life, such as studies, work, or relationships, it takes the form of episodic acute stress. Episodic stress is a continuous feeling that surrounds them with nervous energy all the time, which can trigger anxiousness, irritability, and short temperament. While stress is often perceived as merely worrying about situations and matters, with this type of stress it is much more. Episodic acute stress is often associated with hostility, which is seen by many as an expression of anger and not stress.

Anxiety

Everyone feels anxiety once in a while. For example, when your heartbeat gets faster before making an important presentation at work. This is a totally normal part of daily functioning and is managed well by most.

Anxiety disorders are a different, albeit, serious ball game. As anxiety disorders worsen, they can become a problem by hampering your ability to function in normal everyday situations. Long term anxiety can also contribute to a range of mental illnesses, including depression. There are many types of anxiety disorders, as discussed below:

Types of Anxiety Disorders

1. Social Anxiety Disorder or Social Phobia:

This kind of anxiety disorder is an anxiety disorder that is characterized by worry or fear of embarrassment in everyday social situations. Social anxiety disorder can be limited to one situation, or it can manifest in a variety of situations like speaking at a gathering or work meeting, or eating in front of another person, or even a fear of being judged on the clothes they wear when meeting people. It is an overwhelming fear that can appear in almost all situations that involve interacting with people. Its symptoms can be experienced in front of one person or many people alike. This can cause a person to become isolated, and avoid social interaction.

2. Generalized Anxiety Disorder (GAD):

Generalized Anxiety Disorder (GAD) can develop in both children and adults alike. It has symptoms similar to other mental disorders, like panic disorder. It is characterized by excessive and unnatural fear for no reason. It manifests through over thinking about plans and events and fearing the worst outcomes for apparently no reason. Another manifestation can be a perception of events as threatening. Other signs of GAD include fear of uncertain situations, inability to cope with worry, failure to relax, indecisiveness, and fear of bad decision making.

Physical symptoms of generalized anxiety disorder may include, but are not limited to, excessive sweating, chronic fatigue, trembling, shivering, nervousness, irritable bowel syndrome, and trouble sleeping.

3. Panic Disorder:

Panic disorder manifests itself through random repeated attacks of panic and fears that peak within minutes, and are characterized through physical symptoms like chest pains that can feel like a heart attack, sweating, shortness of breath, hot flashes, lightheadedness, palpitations, and numbing. Its psychological symptoms may include fear of dying, abandonment, or detachment.

Panic attacks are usually unexpected, and during the attack, one or more than one above mentioned symptoms can occur concurrently. A panic attack can last for 20 minutes or more, and usually peaks in intensity at around ten minutes or so.

4. Obsessive Compulsive Disorder (OCD):

OCD is an anxiety disorder where a person has displays long-term, uncontrollable, repetitive obsessions and behaviors. Its symptoms include fear of germs or dirt, compulsive thoughts about religion, ideologies or sex, aggressive thoughts towards other people, and an obsession with symmetry or order. Compulsion can manifest itself in obsessive cleaning, rearranging of things, and repeatedly checking or doing things. These symptoms can come and go. It's common for them to be excessive at first before dimming for a period of time, and then increasing in intensity once again. This anxiety disorder is common among children and adults alike.

5. Post-Traumatic Stress Disorder (PTSD):

Post-Traumatic stress disorder (PTSD) can occur in adults and children at least one month after they experience a traumatic event. The kind of event that causes PTSD is the one where there is a perceived or actual danger to a person's physical or psychological well-being. Traumatic events that can start the PTSD often include exposure to war, accidents, or sexual violence. A person can experience PTSD through direct exposure to a traumatic event, witnessing the disturbing experience, learning about the disturbing event related to a close family member or relative, or exposure to traumatic details by responders to the event.

6. Other Specific Phobias:

Anxiety disorder can manifest itself in many phobias that can include things like a fear of heights or traveling. These types of fears differ from ordinary fear in the sense that they seem out of proportion and may affect the daily functioning of a person.

Causes of Anxiety

Anxiety can have many causes. They can be divided into:

1. Genetics:

According to research, if anxiety disorder starts at a young age, that is before the age of 20, then it is probably in your genes. Genetics can play an important role in making a person vulnerable to anxiety. Genetic disposition, like having a family member with anxiety, can increase risk factors for anxiety in a person.

2. Environment:

Environmental factors can play an important role in the development of anxiety disorders. The foremost environmental factor is stress. If you are experiencing stress as a result of relationships, work, family, health, or any other area of life, it can cause anxiety. Stress-related anxiety can spiral into more destructive behaviors, like drug abuse, alcohol abuse, and other addictive behaviors.

However, it should be kept in mind that normal day to day stress is different from the stress that causes anxiety. Although normal stress can occur, it will not stop you from carrying on with tasks, whereas stress-related anxiety can hamper normal day to day functioning and can manifest into severe physical symptoms.

3. Medical Reasons:

There can be numerous medical causes for anxiety-related disorders. Conversely, anxiety disorders themselves can lead to other medical issues. Here are a few of the things that can cause, or are caused by, anxiety disorders:

- Medications

Some medications have side effects that can cause anxiety attacks. Many over-the-counter weight loss supplements have been known to cause anxiety as an unpleasant side effect. Ingredients like guarana and ephedra often create anxiety in people. Medications for the thyroid gland and asthma drugs can also have side effects that can put people at risk of developing a serious anxiety disorder.

- Heart Disease:

Constant anxiety can lead to heart disease. People with generalized anxiety disorder (GAD) are prone to the risks of cardiovascular diseases. Physical symptoms of anxiety may include heart palpitations and dryness of the mouth. These symptoms also occur before and after a heart attack, and can last longer in women.

- Thyroid Gland:

The thyroid gland is a gland that regulates the metabolism and energy levels in the human body. Anxiety symptoms that include weight loss, dizziness, and heat intolerance can be due to a malfunctioning thyroid gland. If you experience any of these symptoms on a regular basis, then you should have your thyroid function tested.

- Caffeine:

Caffeine is a stimulant that can cause anxiety. Caffeine's effect on an anxiety-prone person can be equal to the effect of a disturbing event. It is, therefore, necessary to keep intake of caffeine to a minimum for people who are at risk of developing an anxiety disorder.

- Unspecified Medical Conditions:

If you feel physical symptoms that are a hallmark of anxiety that you cannot explain and are persistent, then it may actually be caused by an underlying undiagnosed illness and should be checked by a doctor.

- Brain Chemistry:

Anxiety disorders can be caused by brain chemistry alterations like altered hormones and electrolyte imbalances in the brain. Brain chemistry can be altered due to both environmental factors and genetics. Such altered brain function can make a person more prone to anxiety triggers.

- Drug or Alcohol Abuse:

There are links that suggest alcohol and drug use can cause anxiety disorders to develop. Drug and alcohol use can alter a person's state of mind. Chronic drug and alcohol abuse can make people two to three times more susceptible to anxiety disorders. Drug and alcohol abuse also seem to worsen the anxiety symptoms, may it be physical or psychological symptoms. On the other hand, alcohol and drug withdrawal can also worsen the anxiety-related symptoms or increase the intensity or recurrence of anxiety attacks. Alcohol and drug abuse can, therefore, make the treatment for anxiety disorders quite difficult due to a vicious repetitive cycle of abuse and anxiety combined.

Prevention and Remedies for Anxiety Disorders

Anyone can suffer from an anxiety disorder, may it be due to genetics, environmental factors, or a host of other reasons. It must be remembered that stressing over your anxiety will only make the symptoms worse for you. Rather than worrying, remedies must be sought. People who suffer from anxiety can be helped through medical attention and counseling. Since untreated anxiety can cause depression and can also manifest itself in other severe and chronic mental illnesses, it's important to seek treatment as soon as possible.

Anxiety attacks can often be prevented through simple actions. Some preventive measures include:

i. Seek help from medical professionals trained in treating/preventing anxiety disorders.
ii. Try to avoid remaining in situations that you know trigger your anxiety.
iii. Undertake physical activities such as exercise as part of your daily routine.

iv. Foster close relationships with family, peers, and friends that offer support and comfort.
v. Avoid using drugs and alcohol, even if it eases your anxiety in the short term.

Masks of Anger

Just like how anxiety is often masked by anger, anger itself can hide quite effectively. The ways that anger is masked can look very different from typical anger and may appear to just be part of one's personality.

Some masks of anger can be:

i. **Aloofness:**
A person may show aloofness from the environment around them and may not show emotions in situations where others normally show emotions. For example, they may remain cold when a loved one leaves.

ii. **Cynicism:**
You may have a friend that is cynical about everything. They may think the glass is not just half empty, it was never and will never be half-filled. This kind of cynicism may be hiding underlying anger.

iii. **Snobbery:**

A snobbish coworker who always puts you down may actually be angry at the world and the injustices they feel have affected them. Snobbery can be a mask for pent up anger.

iv. **Frustration:**

Frustration is often actually a way people mask the anger of not meeting their expectations.

v. **Sarcasm**

Sarcasm is a common way of deflecting anger management issues. Pay attention to any overly sarcastic friends, as they may be struggling with anger issues and need your support and help.

vi. **Self-Pity**

Some people are always cloaked in self-pity. They may gloat about how they have been deprived of their rights. Self-pity can be a mask for anger at times as well.

vii. **Sadness**

Anger can also show itself in the form of sadness. Anger at not meeting expectations can result in a person withdrawing from other people and the world. For example, anger at not being able to stop a partner from leaving can present itself as sadness.

viii. Arrogance

Many arrogant people may just be arrogant as a personality trait; however, some may be hiding underlying anger. They may use arrogance as a shield or a defense mechanism against getting hurt and resultantly getting angry.

ix. Guilt:

Guilt can also show itself as a mask for anger. You might feel guilty for not being a good parent when your child gets bad grades, and mask this anger as guilt and vice versa.

x. Resentment:

Resentment most often hides anger. You may be angry that your well-deserved promotion went to another person and mask your anger in that situation with resentment.

xi. Self-righteousness:

Many self-righteous people are just angry at things around them and hide it under the guise of self-righteousness. For example, some hardcore preachers may have anger towards a certain practice and make it a point to create a self-righteous attitude around their dislike towards that certain practice.

Chapter 6: Solving Problems without Getting Angry

At one point or another in life, we all have felt totally irritated while in a professional environment or at home. For example, let's imagine you worked day and night on a project only for your boss to totally dismiss your efforts and ideas. In this situation, feeling irritated would be a totally understandable response. As discussed earlier, anger can be a normal and even a healthy emotion, but the important thing you need to learn is how to control and alleviate your anger in a positive way. Uncontrolled anger is going to take control of both your health and your relationships at the workplace and at home.

To manage anger or solve problems without getting angry, you must focus on the following two factors:

Self-control – Self-control plays an important role when it comes to anger management. Giving an instant reaction is easy; however, putting some thought into your actions can save you from situations that may cause feelings of displeasure. It only takes a few seconds to decide how to react appropriately instead of making an instant reaction that you may regret later. Cultivating this self-control is highly important when it comes to solving problems without losing becoming angry.

Self-awareness – Self-awareness allows you to evaluate what you are thinking and how it can affect you or your surroundings. Young children aren't really aware of their feelings or why they feel a certain way; they just behave as they feel without putting any thought into it. In comparison, adults have the control and mental capability to think before acting and expressing their opinions. When you feel angry thoughts starting to develop, take a step back and take note of your feelings and what may be causing these thoughts, before reacting in an inappropriate manner.

Self-control and self-awareness, in combination, enable you to better deal with anger, anxiety, and depression.

In this chapter we are going to explore these five important aspects of anger management:

1. How to keep your cool while solving problems

2. Problem-solving skills

3. Dealing with anger before it ruins your home life

4. Dealing with anger before it affects your professional life

5. How problem-solving skills help with depression and anxiety

How to Keep Your Cool While Solving Problems

When times get difficult in life and we are faced with complicated problems, it can be hard to stay motivated and moving forward. The following points will help you to understand how to keep your cool, stay positive, and stay motivated when things are going badly:

Remain Calm under Pressure

The starting point for staying calm while solving problems is that you refuse to react in a sudden and fierce way. Instead, take a deep breath and relax your mind to think carefully about your next move. This may sound impossible for those who face strong aggression but with regular practice, one can get hold of their impulses and react in a more appropriate and calculated manner.

Tell Yourself to Accept the Problem

You first need to accept the problem that you may have, before trying to solve it. This will allow you to stop unnecessary energy into the problem. Simply complaining that a problem exists without accepting it as a fact can make the problem look bigger than it actually is which can be overwhelming. Failing to accept the existence of a problem also makes it much harder to find a solution for it.

Pay Attention to the Problem

Ask yourself what is causing the problem in the given situation? For example, the problem could be being caused by pressure at work.

Then ask, what you can do to change the situation to make it more favorable for yourself? In this example you could talk to your boss about having a more manageable workload.

Finally, ask yourself what are the hurdles in your way of solving your problem? In this situation it might be that your work is understaffed, or that your boss in unreasonable.

After answering these questions, you can use your answers to plan a proper solution and create ways to overcome the hurdles that are hindering your progress. Once you have a plan, it's a lot easier to remain calm and not feel overwhelmed by a situation.

Ask Yourself: What is the worst thing that could have happened?

Instead of overreacting, remain calm and ask yourself, "What's the worst thing that could have happened?" Listen patiently to yourself and search for the answer. The process of evaluating the problem by asking such questions will allow you to feel relaxed and more confident that things aren't as bad as they could be.

Stay Positive and Try to Figure out a Possible Solution along the Way

In stressful situations, you may feel lost and your mind may linger on thousands of thoughts while looking for the right solution for your problems. In the process, some of your thoughts might turn negative based on your unpleasant past experiences, or assumptions that you may hold about the future. The more that you focus on these negative thoughts, the more real they will feel, and the more frustrated and stressed you will become. It is essential to put your focus on the positive aspects as much as possible and dismiss the negative thoughts when they arise.

Develop an Unbreakable Solution Plan

Discipline yourself to remain "solution-oriented" no matter how tough your circumstances become. Always try to find a solution for your depression and anger, no matter what.

When you study workplace stress closely, you will see that someone's stress often rises the moment they switch from a solution focus to a problem focus. To remain solution focused is a tough job, yet if done properly it can save you from unwanted episodes of anger.

Step into Another Person's Shoes

The next time you find yourself stuck and facing a challenge, ask yourself, "What would someone you admire do in such a situation?" Do what you envision they would do when they go face a similar problem.

Contextualize Your Anger and Redefine Failure

Take a step back and ask yourself exactly what is causing your depression and anger. Humans often dramatize things that do not need to be dramatized. In identifying the cause of your emotions, you will likely realize that they aren't as bad as you first thought. Once you have an understanding of the problem, you can begin to view it less as something to be angry over, and regard it more so as a mere obstacle with which you have to deal. Find a lesson within the problem aim to remain calm. This will take practice and time since managing anger requires a certain level of self-motivation and willpower.

Trust Yourself

Above anything else, self-trust is important. At some point, you may feel that everything is going against you, and that your life plans are being affected negatively. In this situation, you must not lose hope, and remain consistent with your efforts. In the process, you may need to change paths to achieve your goal, but that doesn't mean that you have failed. You have just opted for plan B to get achieve your desired goals. Changing plans without a loss of enthusiasm involves a certain level of trust in yourself.

Stop Demanding Perfection

Finally, stop demanding perfection for yourself, because you are not perfect, and neither is anyone else. And that's totally okay! We all fail to control our anger and depression sometimes and no one expects us to get things right 100% all the time. Instead of shooting for perfection, simply aim to do better each day than you did yesterday.

Problem Solving Skills

What are problem-solving skills and how they can help us in dealing with different areas of life?

Problem-solving skills help you find the source of a problem and then allow you to determine an effective solution for it. There are also other related skills that can contribute to problem-solving.

Required Skills for Effective Problem-Solving

The act of problem-solving may seem quite simple initially; however, many people feel clueless and find it difficult to identify their own problems and solve them effectively. Successful problem solvers require an important skill set that allows them to deal with their anger problems in an efficient manner from initiation till implementation.

Some of these abilities include; active listening, team building, decision making, communication skills, analysis, research, and creativity.

Research and Analysis

The first step to solve any problem is to start with research and analyze the situation. As a problem solver, you should be able to understand the root cause of the issue that's been bothering you. You can begin by gathering important information about a problem by acquiring knowledge through online research, brainstorming with other team members, or consulting with more experienced colleagues. Using analytical skills during research helps you to distinguish between effective and ineffective solutions.

Decision Making and Communication Process

Ultimately, you will need to make a decision about how to solve problems that arise in front of you. Sometimes, a situation arises wherein you have to make a decision quickly. Strong analytical skills can help you to make appropriate decisions in these situations.

While identifying possible solutions, you need to know how to communicate the problem to others. Using effective communication skills is vital when trying to find a perfect solution in a timely manner.

How can we improve our Problem-Solving Skills?

You can use a variety of methods to improve your problem-solving skills. Below are a few of the methods you may want to try:

Gain knowledge related to your field - Depending upon the industry you work in; increased knowledge will make it easier for you to deal with problems that are related to your work domain. Knowledge gained through research and training can be helpful.

Putting yourself into new situations – You can place yourself in new situations in order to assess and work on your problem-solving skills in a variety of environments. For example, you could volunteer for something that you haven't done before, or embark on a new project.

Take note of others and see how they solve problems – Observe your co-workers and peers who are good at solving problems. You can look for the ways your coworkers adapt to solve their problems. You can apply the same strategies to solve your own problems. Don't hesitate in asking relevant questions that may help you in paving the way for the growth of your problem-solving abilities.

Creative Thinking Skills to Solve Problems

The creative thinking skills used to solve problems consist of these four key elements:

Fluency - generates new ideas

Flexibility - produces a broad range of ideas

Originality - generates uncommon ideas

Elaboration - develops upon ideas

Four Important Stages of Problem-Solving

To effectively deal with a problem, you may need to keep in mind the following steps:

1. Correct Identification of the Problem:

This stage involves the identification and recognition of the problem and accepting that the problem exists. In this phase, you will be required to invest time into the process of analyzing your own thoughts. Pinpointing the exact problem may come as a major task for some, but with consistent questioning and evaluation of one's self, the problem will be identified.

You can ask yourself a set of questions, such as the following, to better analyze the situation:

Is there an underlying problem behind my anger or the way I feel? What is the intensity and nature of that problem? What's the best explanation of my problem? Can I define it?

By investing some time in defining and understanding the problem you will not only be able to identify other associated problems, but also be able to comprehend the nature of the problem from different perspectives.

2. Structure of the Identified Problem:

This step involves careful analysis, strong observation, and overall inspection of the problem so that a clear picture can be drafted of the identified problem.

This step is all about acquiring fact-based information regarding your problem, including what factors have caused the problem, and which past experiences may have been adding to the severity of your anger caused by the problem. The bigger your problem is, the more facets it will likely have.

3. Implement the Solution:

The third step involves both the planning and execution of a solution. The two phases here are input and output.

Input – identify the problem and create a list of possible solutions.
Output - pick a solution from the list and implement it.

4. Review the Results:

The final phase of problem-solving is concerned with the success of the process or solution that you have selected for the problem. Determine whether or not your chosen solution was effective, and if not, identify the reasons why. From there, you can go back to step 3, and select an alternative solution to implement.

Approaching your problems in this logical and calculated manner makes them much easier to deal with. This allows you to remain on top of your problems and gain a sense of control over your life. All of that leads to better control of your emotions, and ultimately, less anxiety, stress, and anger.

Dealing with Anger before It Ruins Your Home Life

The reason behind the anger could be a wide variety of things, for instance, you might have had a tough day at work, a fight with your significant other, or be facing financial stress. All of these things can cause anger on their own, not to mention if they are all experienced on the same day! Regardless of the cause of your anger, you need to calm yourself when faced with such situations, particularly when you're at home. It's common for people with anger issues to unfairly take out their anger on their loved ones at home, who often played no role in causing the anger in the first place.

Try implementing the following strategies to deal with your anger before it has a chance to affect your home life:

Recognize your Triggering Points - You should identify the warning signs of things that make you annoyed. Once you recognize them, you can do your best to avoid such situations, or if unavoidable, implement techniques to relax, such as deep breathing, or progressive muscle relaxation.

Let it go - You should not keep rehashing the incident that made you mad. If there's nothing you can do in the moment to change things, then there's no point in focusing on it. Instead, try focusing on the positive things in your life that you appreciate.

Think Logically – By thinking about your frustrations with logic, your anger will often appear to be irrational, and unfounded. Try looking at your stress and anger logically when it arises, and you'll often find that your feelings of anger aren't actually justified.

Stop Expecting and Start Requesting – If you expect something and it doesn't happen as per your expectations, you can become irritated. If things don't pan out exactly as you envisioned, try not to be upset about it. Instead, communicate your expectations, and make your requests clear to those around you.

Relax – Taking time to unwind and relax is a great way to combat angry feelings. Try implementing the following strategies in your life to help you to de-stress:

- Deep Breathing; breathing into your belly, rather than your chest. Practice taking slow, controlled breaths.
- Start visualizing an imaginary relaxing experience from your memory, such as walking along a beautiful beach.
- Muscle Relaxing exercises such as PMR to reduce tension.

Improve your Communication Skills – People often jump to conclusions when they are angry and say unkind things that come into their mind without thinking. Try to stop and listen before reacting. Take some time to think carefully about how you should respond.

Get Active and Avoid Your Triggers – To avoid anger at home, you can engage in regular physical exercise. This can help to control your anger by burning off extra energy and releasing feel-good endorphins into your body.

You cannot completely avoid angry feelings all the time, but you can minimize them by making some changes to your behavior and the environment in which you live. Purposely avoid events that trigger your anger if possible. Make sure that you get plenty of rest, and always take time to think carefully before responding out of rage.

Dealing with Anger Before it Affects Your Professional Life

All of us have been in a situation where we were not able to control our emotions and anger. When this happens in your personal life, you can react to such situations by shouting or hiding in a corner. However, engaging in these kinds of behavior would be highly inappropriate in the workplace, and as such, you must find different ways to deal with anger when on the job.

Dealing with a Stressful Event at Work

A lot of situations can be stressful in the workplace. For example, facing salary cuts, department changes, or staff layoffs can cause a lot of anxiety. You can hide your emotions in such circumstances or channel them in ways that don't affect your professional life. Employers value staff who can control their anger, perform well even under pressure, and who don't violate the ethics of the office environment.

How to Manage a Stressful Situation at the Workplace

It is important for you to choose how to react to unfavorable situations and negativity around you. People don't need anger management therapy to control their positive emotions as these emotions don't have any negative effects on others. If you can focus on sharing positive emotions professionally, your colleagues will enjoy working alongside you.

However, we don't only experience positive emotions in life, and that's particularly true for life at work. If we want to be valued by our colleagues, we must know how to properly control the anger we may feel. If someone expresses their feelings of anger or frustration in a destructive or unhealthy way, everyone around them suffers. People might be afraid to say anything that might cause a conflict, so they will tread on eggshells around you. This can cause lowered morale, communication, and productivity in the office. All of these things are detrimental in the workplace, so learning to control your anger is a must!

If you are in a workplace that is negatively affected by people's anger issues, there are several things you can do to improve the situation, as discussed below:

Build a Culture for your Workplace – This may involve looking at your recruitment process. Focus on hiring people who have a positive attitude at work and friendly behavior. Having positive people around promotes positivity in others.

Conversely, having negative people only serves to promote negativity.

Well-Behaved Leaders – As they are the senior staff, their behavior influences others in the group. Calm and composed leaders set a good example for everyone as to what professional behavior looks like.

Disciplinary Procedures – There might be staff at your workplace that act unprofessionally. To deter this behavior, you should set some rules and disciplinary procedures. Consequences must exist if they are not able to control their conduct.

Train Your Staff – Everyone should know how to respond to a confrontational situation, and they should report the behavior to senior staff. They need to understand how to deescalate situations and take disciplinary action.

Keep Records – Every incident must be recorded as it enables you to apply disciplinary actions much more professionally.

Don't Take It Personally – Usually, anger issues are developed as a result of past experiences. Anger is their way of dealing with such situations. Stay safe from physically aggressive behavior and avoid escalating the anger of a person who appears to be threatening. It's important that you understand that you are probably not the cause of the person's anger, and that they are facing other problems in their life that are making them behave in this way.

Be Understanding & Empathetic – You should find the root of the problem causing people to have anger issues. Try to understand what is causing their behavior by asking questions and listening to them patiently. Then, you can work with them to find a solution.

How Problem-Solving Skills Help with Depression and Anxiety

Problems seem to look bigger when you are depressed or anxious. The best and the most suitable way to handle them is to break down things into tiny steps. This step-by-step approach to problem-solving can help tremendously in overcoming the challenges that you face.

Understand the problem:

The most important step is to clearly identify what the problem is. For your own convenience, you should note down the problems that you are currently dealing with. Start with the simplest one that you feel confident you can solve.

Then, you will have to ask yourself some questions in order to handle the problem at hand:

1. What exactly is happening to you?
2. Why does it happen?
3. Are there any particular events associated with it?
4. When and where does the problem occur?
5. Who (if anyone) is causing this problem?
6. Why is it difficult for you to handle this problem?

Now, answer each of the questions in your list and assign honest answers to each one of them.

Find Out the Key Factors:

After you have a clearly defined problem, you can decide on the possible solutions available to solve it by using the following steps:

- Use the list of answers that you previously made.
- Jot down all the possible ways you could potentially solve the problem.

- Use your creativity to bring new ideas to the table.
- Write down all the ideas that come to your mind, no matter how childish they may seem.
- Don't evaluate your ideas until you are done with making the list.

Once you are done brainstorming all the possible solutions, make sure to apply the most relevant solutions to your problem. You can start with one solution and if it doesn't work, you can move to another solution from the list.

Make a Strategy:

Lastly, you can form the solutions into a strategized plan. The plan should answer the following questions:

1. What things do you need to move forward with your plan?
2. Do you need anyone to help you achieve your plan? If yes, who?
3. What is the date you wish to have completed your plan?
4. What things will tell you that your problem has been resolved?

Once you've made your strategy, it's time to put it into action.

Executing the strategy:

At this stage, you can implement your plan. When you start implementation, take some time to analyze and critically review your plan. Take note of what worked for you and what didn't, and what things could have been done differently.

If your plan didn't work out, then use the review you did for the plan to make necessary changes. Once your plan has proven successful, celebrate your success and start working on the next problem on the list that you wrote down earlier.

Problem-Solving Therapy for Depression

Problem-Solving Therapy is basically a treatment that helps you take positive actions to fight against the problems in your life. This form of therapy teaches you to proactively solve problems.

Unlike traditional psychotherapy, problem-solving therapy makes use of cognitive and behavioral interventions, helping people directly work on life's challenges.

Problem-solving therapy can also help with achieving goals, finding purpose, reducing depression, managing anxiety, and solving relationship problems. It has been the subject of recent scientific research, showing it can be helpful not only with psychological problems, but with physical illness as well. If you're faced with depression alongside anger issues, this may be a therapy that you wish to explore further.

Conclusion

Thanks again for taking the time to read this book!

You should now have a good understanding of anger, what causes it, and how it can be managed when it gets out of control.

Remember to always consult with a medical professional before undergoing any treatment plan or taking any medication.

I hope you found this book to be helpful in better understanding anger issues, and how they can be managed and overcome.

References

1. Williams, J. (2015). The Amygdala: Definition, Role & Function - Video & Lesson Transcript | Study.com. Retrieved from https://study.com/academy/lesson/the-amygdala-definition-role-function.html
2. Mintz, S. (2019). Fight or Flight Response. Retrieved from https://www.ethicssage.com/2019/02/fight-or-flight-response.html
3. Cherry, K. (2019). The Fight-or-Flight Response Prepares Your Body to Take Action. Retrieved from https://www.verywellmind.com/what-is-the-fight-or-flight-response-2795194
4. Reilly, P., & Scott Shopshire, M. (2014). Anger management for substance abuse and mental health clients: A cognitive behavioral therapy manual. Retrieved from https://www.researchgate.net/publication/277719312_Anger_management_for_substance_abuse_and_mental_health_clients_A_cognitive_behavioral_therapy_manual_DHHS_Pub_No_SMA_02-3661
5. Bushman, B., Baumeister, R., & Stack, A. (1999). Catharsis, Aggression, and Persuasive Influence: Self-Fulfilling or Self-Defeating Prophecies? Retrieved from https://pdfs.semanticscholar.org/12a3/a6701720c1516a5acdec2a3527e2892b3add.pdf

6. Deng, Y., Chang, L., Yang, M., Huo, M., & Zhou, R. (2016). Gender Differences in Emotional Response: Inconsistency between Experience and Expressivity. Retrieved from https://journals.plos.org/plosone/article?id=10.1371/journal.pone.0158666
7. Kross, E., Berman, M., Mischel, W., Smith, E., & Wager, T. (2011). Social rejection shares somatosensory representations with physical pain. Retrieved from https://www.pnas.org/content/pnas/108/15/6270.full.pdf
8. Varvogli, L., & Darviri, C. (2011). Stress Management Techniques: evidence-based procedures that reduce stress and promote health. Retrieved from http://citeseerx.ist.psu.edu/viewdoc/download?doi=10.1.1.851.7680&rep=rep1&type=pdf
9. Gedge, R. (2009). Retrieved from World Wide Web on 12th October 2009 from www.scu.edu.au.
10. Zaidi, U. (2014). Clinical Anger, Affective and Somatic Symptoms in Depressed Patients. Retrieved from http://www.ijstr.org/final-print/dec2014/Clinical-Anger-Affective-And-Somatic-Symptoms-In-Depressed-Patients.pdf

www.ingramcontent.com/pod-product-compliance
Lightning Source LLC
LaVergne TN
LVHW011716060526
838200LV00051B/2913